WELCOME TO REGENCY BRITAIN

By the end of 1810, Britain stood at a crossroads. King George III, after 50 years on the throne, had descended into permanent insanity. His son, George, Prince of Wales, was subsequently appointed as Prince Regent under the Regency Act of 1811. This marked the beginning of a period that became one of the most fascinating and transformative in British history.

The Regency era was a time of flourishing art and culture, with literary icons such as Jane Austen and William Wordsworth, and artists such as John Constable, creating some of their most memorable works. Meanwhile, the Prince Regent's lavish and scandalous lifestyle embodied the spirit of the age, known for its dazzling balls, elegant fashion and romance. Yet, behind all this glitz and glamour, the nation grappled with political turmoil, domestic discontent, war and a thriving criminal underworld. In the *Book of Regency Britain*, join us as we delve into the complex reality of this iconic era.

CONTENTS

SOCIETY & SCANDAL

008 THE MADNESS OF KING GEORGE
George III's struggles with mental illness launched Britain into a glittering Regency

012 THE PRINCE OF PLEASURE
Explore the Prince Regent's extravagant lifestyle and the legacy he left behind

016 THE QUEEN OF HEARTS
Learn all about the Prince Regent's doomed marriage to Caroline of Brunswick

022 THE ORIGINAL PEOPLE'S PRINCESS
Princess Charlotte of Wales's tragic death plunged the nation into mourning

030 HOW TO 'MAKE IT' IN REGENCY LONDON
Discover our guide to surviving the social season in one piece

036 RUNNING AWAY TO GRETNA GREEN
Find out why Regency Britain saw such a boom in scandalous elopements

038 REGENCY STYLE
Unravel the elegant and iconic fashions that defined the era

044 SCANDAL, SATIRE AND THE PRESS
Uncover the rise of the press and tabloids in the Regency era

048 SEX, LIES AND DUELS
Explore the scandals that besmirched the great and good of Regency Britain

050 THE REGENCY UNDERWORLD
Expose the shadowy world of crime that lurked behind the glitz and glamour

POLITICS & POWER

056 THE TORIES IN POWER
Uncover the turbulent years of Regency politics against a backdrop of national discontent

060 MURDER OF THE PRIME MINISTER
How Spencer Perceval lost his life at the hands of a vengeful murderer

062 REMEMBERING PETERLOO
Experts discuss the importance of keeping the memory of Peterloo alive

070 BRITAIN AT WAR
Explore the military conflicts that dominated the Regency period

074 BATTLE OF WATERLOO
Inside the battle that finally brought an end to the Napoleonic Wars

078 THE WAR ON SLAVERY
Learn about the fight for abolition during the Georgian era

036

CULTURE & KNOWLEDGE

082 CLASS AND ENTERTAINMENT
Discover the contrasts between classes in Regency Britain

088 NO HOLDS BARRED
The blood-spattered truth behind Britain's underground fight club

094 JANE AUSTEN
Take a journey through the life and works of the iconic author

098 THE YEAR WITHOUT SUMMER
Dive into the competition that birthed a masterpiece of English literature

102 LITERARY ICONS
Meet some of the greatest writers of Regency Britain and their significant works

106 REGENCY ARTISTS
Everything you need to know about the height of the Romanticism movement

110 THE GRAND TOUR
Join the young aristocrats who journeyed across the continent in search of classic art and culture

116 A TOUR OF REGENCY ENGLAND
Take a walk through some of the era's most-loved locations

120 THE INDUSTRIAL REVOLUTION
Find out how developments in science and technology changed Britain forever

124 DOCTOR'S ORDERS
Step into the waiting room and uncover the brutal treatments of the Regency era

126 REGENCY DISCOVERY AND INNOVATION
Learn about the inventions and discoveries that excited Regency Britain

CONTENTS

"Despite his reputation for greed, womanising and laziness, his influence during the Regency era fostered a remarkable cultural flourishing"

012

094

110

022

074

102

5

SOCIETY & SCANDAL

008 **THE MADNESS OF KING GEORGE**

012 **THE PRINCE OF PLEASURE**

016 **THE QUEEN OF HEARTS**

022 **THE ORIGINAL PEOPLE'S PRINCESS**

030 **HOW TO MAKE IT IN REGENCY LONDON**

036 **RUNNING AWAY TO GRETNA GREEN**

038 **REGENCY STYLE**

044 **SCANDAL, SATIRE AND THE PRESS**

048 **SEX, LIES AND DUELS**

050 **THE REGENCY UNDERWORLD**

SOCIETY & SCANDAL

THE MADNESS OF KING GEORGE

King George III, remembered as the Mad King, lost his wits and his power, launching Great Britain into a glittering Regency

WRITTEN BY **CATHERINE CURZON**

King George III and Queen Charlotte were crowned in 1761. Pious, modest and fond of the quiet life, the couple were seemingly immune to scandal; unique among the Georgian kings, he didn't even take a mistress. Yet George's turbulent reign ended in tragedy.

George's first brush with the illness that would eventually overwhelm him came in 1765, when the heavily pregnant Queen nursed him through a severe fever. This brief episode led to conversations between King and Parliament regarding a Regency Bill, which would come into force should the monarch ever be too ill to rule. With no other obvious candidates, it was decided in theory that the regent would be Charlotte. Unlike the doughty queen in *Bridgerton*, she loathed the idea; George had always encouraged her to be a domestic partner, not a politician, and that was just how she liked it.

In the years that followed, the royal family was beset by domestic drama. The two youngest princes, one-year-old Alfred, and four-year-old Octavius, died within six months of one another, plunging the King into a deep depression. On top of that, George IV - the Prince of Wales and the King's eldest son and heir - ran wild as soon as he came of age, The hellraising Prince was a constant thorn in the King's side, and was something his already frayed nerves simply couldn't endure.

In 1788, George was struck down by terrible stomach pains that his doctors put down to stress. A trip to take the waters at Cheltenham Spa seemed to rejuvenate the ailing king but as soon as he returned to Kew after a few weeks, the pain returned, alongside violent mood swings and an angry rash. In one of his lucid moments, he advised his wife to prepare for the worst.

Feverish and sleepless, George foamed at the mouth and spoke in rambling sentences that left his family terrified. Suspicious that the Prince of Wales was conspiring to seize power, George attacked him at a family dinner, causing Charlotte to gather up her daughters and flee. The King was placed in isolation, growing hysterical when he glimpsed his wife and children from the window but was unable to reach them.

Eventually, Charlotte called in Lincolnshire physician, Dr Francis Willis, who was famed for his ability to cure madness. Dr Willis immediately confined his patient to the White House at Kew, once George's favourite family home. Here he was

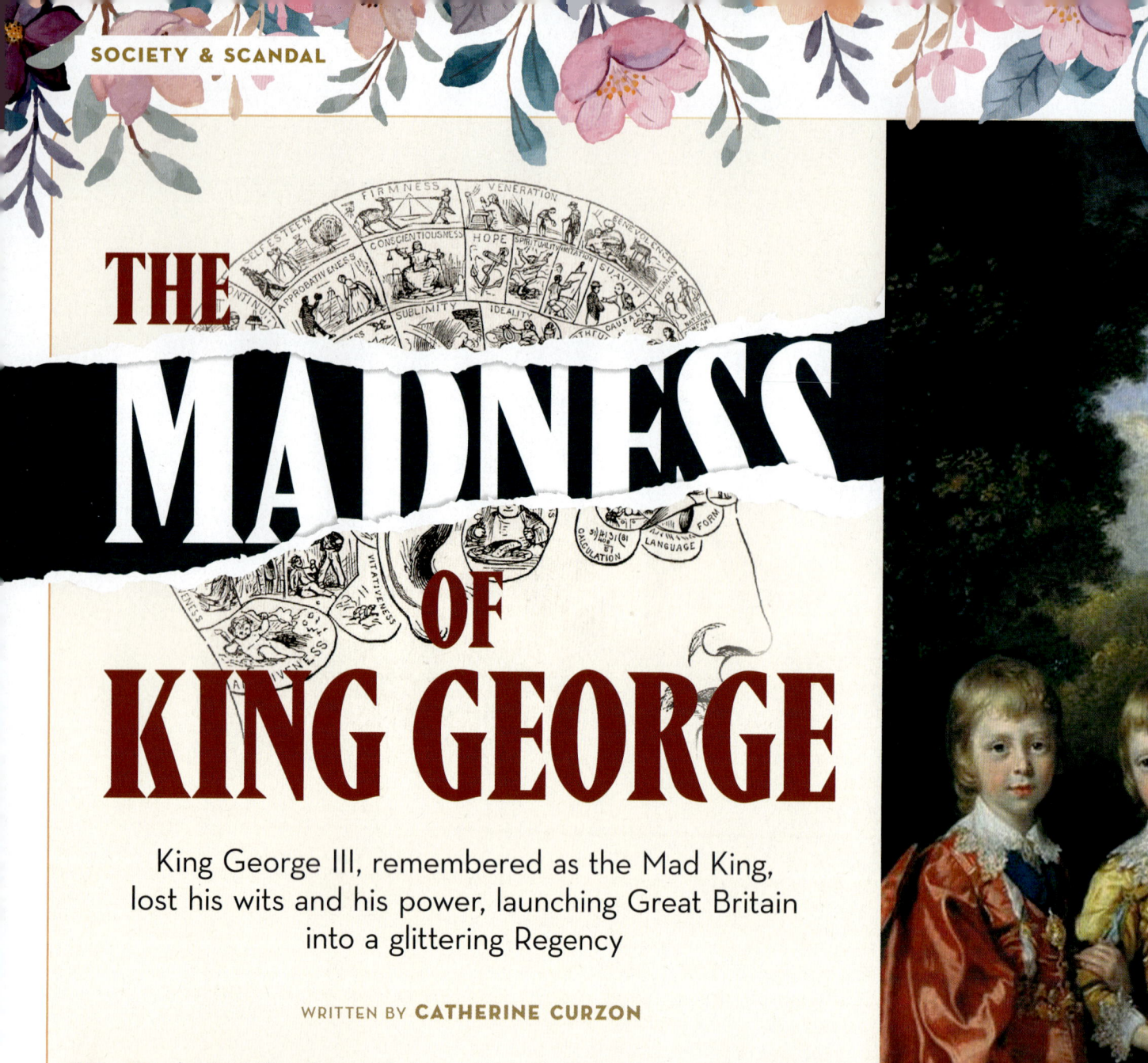

King George III and Queen Charlotte hoped for a quiet life with their children; sadly, fate had other plans in store

THE MADNESS OF KING GEORGE

SOCIETY & SCANDAL

straightjacketed and gagged, then fed potions to encourage vomiting and diarrhoea in the belief that they would purge the illness. Should George complain, he was strapped into the infamous 'Coronation Chair', a restraining device that held him fast until he submitted to Dr Willis. The doctor's regime appears brutal, but at the time his ice baths, leeches, blisters and forced purges were seen as progressive.

It was clear that the cure would not come overnight: the Regency Bill was back on the table. This time, the Whig opposition argued that the only candidate for the role of regent could be the Prince of Wales. Tory prime minister, Pitt the Younger, agreed in theory, but feared that the Prince would kick his party out of power and replace them with the Whigs. Only when a clause prohibiting this – along with another making Charlotte responsible for the King's household and care – was included did work on the Regency Bill continue. The Prince of Wales would not get his hands on the royal coffers.

Negotiations over the Regency Bill dragged on for so long that the King's sudden recovery overtook them. He grew lucid and his physical symptoms resolved until supervised visits with his beloved dog were allowed, followed by walks with Charlotte and little Princess Amelia. By the time the Regency Bill entered the debate stage in early 1789, it was no longer necessary. Dr Willis was lauded as the King's saviour but the illness had most likely simply resolved on it its own.

Then in 1801, the fever returned. Dr Willis was summoned, and George was once again confined to the White House, but this time he threatened to go on strike from all his official duties. A deal was struck by which George was allowed to see his family and take a restorative trip to Weymouth, but there was one last thing the King had to do. Perhaps tormented by memories of the punishments doled out at Kew, George had the White House torn down. The place where he had once played with his children and lived his happiest memories had become his hell. Charlotte promised that none of the Willis family would ever treat him again.

George relapsed in 1804 and his sons, the Dukes of Cumberland and Kent, summoned Dr Samuel Foart Simmons, of St Luke's Hospital for Lunatics, who straightjacketed, blistered and gagged the King. Wrongly believing Charlotte was to blame for this, the King rejected her completely, instead declaring that he loved her friend, Lady Pembroke. Yet George would also attempt to seize his wife, leaving her so frightened that she refused to be alone with him.

This time, there would be no miracle recovery, and George's health declined at an alarming rate. He spent his days in his rooms at Windsor, across the courtyard from the chamber where Princess Amelia languished with tuberculosis. By now almost blind, each afternoon George was helped to her bedside and father and daughter would spend hours together in conversation, prayer or simply silent contemplation. Knowing that she would soon die, Amelia commissioned a mourning ring for her father. The ring contained a lock of Amelia's hair and was inscribed with her name and the words, "Remember me". The King sobbed as she slid the ring onto his finger and told her, "You are engraven on my heart".

Amelia died in November 1810, aged 27. With her loss, George was plunged into a madness from which he would never recover. The day after Amelia's death, he was straightjacketed; within a week, the Cabinet imposed a visit by Dr Robert Willis, son of Francis, against the wishes of the royal family. It was no longer a question of if there would be a Regency Bill, but when.

From this moment, protecting George became Charlotte's focus. When Dr Willis confirmed that there was no hope of a recovery, the prime minister, Spencer Perceval, drew up the basics of the Regency Bill that gave Queen Charlotte complete responsibility for the care of the King. The Prince of Wales was appointed Prince Regent on 5 February 1811; contrary to Tory fears, he did not dismiss their administration.

The Prince Regent, later to reign as George IV, assumed the reins of power when his father was too ill to continue

Dr Francis Willis's brutal treatments terrorised the King, who feared him above all others

THE MADNESS OF KING GEORGE

When the King lost his children, Alfred, Octavius, and his beloved Amelia, the impact on his mental health was catastrophic

The Modern Diagnosis

Modern doctors have their own thoughts on exactly what caused King George III's madness

Though George's doctors put his diagnosis down to stress and mania, modern medics have come up with their own diagnoses for the King. In 1966, doctors Ida Macalpine and Richard Hunter put forward the theory that he was suffering with a metabolic condition, specifically the liver disease porphyria, which seemed to align with all his symptoms including occasional reports of discoloured urine. This became the widely accepted diagnosis until 2005, when it was further bolstered by a study on a lock of George III's hair, which revealed high levels of arsenic, a possible cause of porphyria.

However, more recently Macalpine and Hunter's conclusions have come increasingly under scrutiny, with modern researchers questioning whether people have been too quick to accept this explanation. Instead, they have suggested that King George III was suffering from a psychiatric disorder, most likely bipolar disorder. Researchers Dr Peter Garrard and Dr Vassiliki Rentoumi carried out an extensive study of the sovereign's letters, identifying both the manic and depressive phases of his condition.

While we will never know for sure, these two approaches to diagnosis: physical versus mental, offer a fascinating insight into the changing nature of diagnoses. Of course, without a patient to examine, the ultimate answer must remain a mystery.

"The doctor's regime appears brutal, but his ice baths, leeches, blisters and forced purges were seen as progressive"

King George III knew nothing of this and though Charlotte continued to administer his care, her husband longer knew his wife. For years, Charlotte and George had been each other's champions, now, tragically, Queen Charlotte could not bear to be in the company of the man who simply didn't recognise her. Queen Charlotte and King George met for the final time in June 1812.

Free of responsibility, George led a quiet life at Windsor Castle, inspecting invisible troops and holding audiences with long dead politicians and courtiers, or chatting merrily with his deceased children. Sometimes he hammered tunelessly at the harpsichord, released from the torturous treatments he had once endured. Now the old king was allowed to indulge himself as he wished; blind, deaf and suffering from dementia, George was content in his world.

In 1818, Queen Charlotte was seized by a desperate need to see her husband one last time, but her failing health meant that she could travel no further than Kew. It was there that she died on 17 November. When her funeral procession reached Windsor Castle, straw was sprinkled in the courtyard to ensure that George knew nothing of the occasion.

King George III died on 29 January 1820. He was laid to rest beside Queen Charlotte and, as had been his wish, the bodies of Octavius and Alfred were placed beside them at Windsor. Sixty long years after his coronation, King George III had found peace at last.

Nothing remains of the White House at Kew; George III had his once-beloved home torn down after it fell into disrepair

Coronation portrait of George IV, painted by Sir Thomas Lawrence, 1821

THE PRINCE OF PLEASURE

The Prince Regent, later King George IV, left a legacy characterised by greed and laziness, yet his reign also saw a flourishing in the worlds of art and culture

WRITTEN BY **EMMA SLATTERY WILLIAMS**

Born into the tumultuous reign of his father, King George III, the Prince battled a dual struggle between familial expectations and personal demons. And despite his reputation for greed, womanising and laziness, his influence during the Regency era fostered a remarkable cultural flourishing that forever changed the landscape of British art and society.

George Augustus Frederick was born in 1762 as the eldest of 15 children born to George III and Charlotte of Mecklenburg-Strelitz. Father and son had something of a strained relationship – the Prince was separated from his family while a young boy to live under the tutelage of Lord Holderness, a particularly strict tutor. The severe regime he lived under, in addition to the feeling of being neglected by his parents, saw him grow up rebellious and unwilling to act in a manner becoming of a future king.

A stream of women would visit his bedchamber throughout his late teens, until he met Mrs Maria Fitzherbert. At just 21 years old he married the twice-widowed Maria in secret, who was six years his senior. This was an unwise move for multiple reasons – he had not sought his father's permission, which he was required to do before the age of 25, and she was Roman Catholic. This was particularly significant because the 1701 Act of Settlement forbade a Catholic or someone with a Catholic spouse from inheriting the throne or marrying an heir. The Catholic Church recognised their marriage as legal, but English law did not.

In 1788 it looked as though George III – who suffered from ill health throughout his life – had taken a turn for the worse and a Regency was proposed. While most of the government believed the Prince of Wales had an automatic right to rule, the prime minister at the time, William Pitt, insisted that for at least the first 12 months he should have limited powers when it came to bestowing certain offices. However, the King soon rallied enough to retain the crown.

As Prince of Wales, George received a generous allowance of £62,000 a year, which came with

The Royal Pavilion, which was designed by John Nash as a seaside pleasure palace for the Prince Regent

SOCIETY & SCANDAL

The Dandy and the Regent

Beau Brummell exemplified the idea of the Regency 'dandy' – upper-class men known for their love of expensive fashion, good manners and who emulated the aristocratic lifestyle. His rise began in the early 1800s, marked by an unparalleled sense of style and understanding of social dynamics, as well as his association with the Prince. Brummell's influence went beyond clothing; he became a trendsetter, championing a more understated, tailored aesthetic that contrasted with the ostentation of his peers.

His relationship with George was complex. Initially, Brummell enjoyed the Prince's favour. The two shared a passion for fashion and the finer things in life, with Brummell often advising George on matters of style and decorum. Their camaraderie epitomised the dandy culture of the time, with Brummell serving as both a confidante and a style guru.

However, their relationship soured as Brummell's outspoken nature and social critiques began to clash with the Prince's increasingly extravagant lifestyle. After a nasty falling out, Brummell fell from grace after calling the Prince 'fat', and he later fled to France to escape his debts. Despite this, his impact on fashion and social etiquette endured, influencing not only the Prince but the broader landscape of British high society.

Mass crowds gathered to attend George IV's coronation in 1821

A caricature of Regency dandy, Beau Brummell by Robert Dighton, 1805

Carlton House on Pall Mall and a household of his own. Here he held a rival court to that of his parents with lavish entertainments and parties. However, two of his greatest desires were prevented by his father – to leave the country without permission and to have a role in the military. His father hoped he would support him in the running of the country, or at the very least stay out of the public eye – something he most definitely did not do. Contemporary caricatures often mocked his behaviour.

The Prince spent money without a care, effortlessly racking up huge debts – from gambling and renovations on his residences, to purchasing extravagant clothes, furniture and art. He was even said to see visitors – both personal and politically – in his bedchamber in an almost state of nudity. Further proof of his reckless nature and wasteful spending was that despite the vast amount of money he poured into Carlton House, it was eventually demolished in 1827.

In exchange for the government paying off the huge debts he had accrued, Prince George agreed to marry his cousin, Princess Caroline of Brunswick, in 1795. This was far from a happy union. He attempted and failed to get out of it, leading to many mistresses over the years – from actresses to the wives of courtiers. Their only child, Princess Charlotte, was born a year after their marriage. She became a beloved member of the Royal Family and the nation's darling.

In addition to loving the finer things in life, George was cultured and a lover of collecting art, contributing much to the Royal Collection as it is today. He gathered paintings, as well as textiles, ceramics and furniture from some of the greatest artists of the day. The priciest painting he ever bought was Rembrandt's *The Shipbuilder and his Wife* (1633) for a record 5,000 guineas. He was an avid collector of the works of prolific Regency portrait artist Sir Thomas Lawrence, so much so that he became his patron.

A Voluptuary Under the Horrors of Digestion, a satirical rendering of Prince George by James Gillray

THE PRINCE OF PLEASURE

Carlton House wasn't the only residence that George spent money on - wanting a home outside the capital, he commissioned John Nash to create an opulent seaside residence for him. The Royal Pavilion in Brighton was completed in 1822 and drew on inspiration from Chinese and Indian architecture. It was transformed from a modest seaside villa to a lavish pleasure palace by the sea - if ever there was a symbol of George's indulgent decadence, this was it.

However, despite his extravagance and perceived greed, there was a softer side to George. He was incredibly skilled at putting people at ease during social occasions, was playful with children and he was a lover of animals. He was known by some as the 'first gentleman of England' due to his charm, manners and kindness. He felt uneasy over the execution of criminals and preferred to show mercy if he could.

Tragedy struck in 1810, when Princess Amelia - the youngest child of George III - died at the age of 27. This was the last straw for the King's fragile mental health, and he never recovered, suffering from blindness and fits of insanity until his death.

On 7 February 1811, the government passed the Regency Act, making George, the Prince of Wales, the Prince Regent - and monarch in everything but name. To celebrate, he held an opulent fete with more than 2,000 guests at Carlton House. Dressed in the uniform of a field-marshal - a position denied him - he entertained members of the exiled French royal family as well as other aristocracy with fireworks and sumptuous meals. The grandeur of the occasion left a sour taste in the mouths of the Prince Regent's critics and the public. The Napoleonic Wars had caused economic hardship and unemployment across Britain and these festivities were viewed as inappropriate.

A lover of excess and vices such as drinking, women and gambling, the Prince Regent was a far cry from his respectable father. George III was not known to keep mistresses, enjoyed collecting books and had a keen interest in agriculture - leading to his nickname, 'farmer George'. The Prince Regent, on the other hand, was seen as lazy, vain, spoilt and self-indulgent, though with impeccable manners and fashion taste, leading to his affectionate moniker of 'Prinny'.

By the time he became king after the death of his father in January 1820, he was 57, overweight and suffering from a dependency to both alcohol and laudanum.

It is therefore no surprise that he preferred to leave the actual ruling to his government, enjoying partying over policy - the role was almost an irritant and inconvenience to him. However, the power and privilege it afforded were welcome, as long as he only had to exert minimal effort.

As a young man and to annoy his father, he'd courted Whig politicians but George turned towards the Tory party as he became older. Against his own convictions, his government pressured him to sign the Catholic Emancipation Bill in 1829, removing the bar on Roman Catholics sitting in Parliament and most public offices.

As his reign progressed, his involvement in government diminished further as he started to seclude himself at Windsor Castle. His lavish lifestyle took its toll on his health - in the later years of his life he was suffering from multiple ailments including gout and cataracts, and would regularly take 100 drops of laudanum for bladder pain so that he could attend state occasions.

On 26 June 1830, he died at the age of 67 after confessing his decadent ways. With no surviving children, George's brother William inherited the throne. *The Times* reflected the public sentiment at his passing: "There never was an individual less regretted by his fellow creatures". Despite his extravagant lifestyle and public discontent, though, George IV's reign undeniably shaped the cultural landscape of Britain.

> *"By the time he became king, he was 57, overweight and suffering from a dependency to both alcohol and laudanum"*

Maria Anne Fitzherbert - the Prince's first long-time companion and who he secretly married in an illegal Catholic ceremony

Carlton House on Pall Mall, George's lavish London home

SOCIETY & SCANDAL

The public loathed the spoiled and capricious prince and rallied behind his wronged and philanthropic wife. They cheered her on as she battled against his efforts to divorce her

THE QUEEN OF HEARTS

When the Prince of Wales married Caroline of Brunswick, things started badly and went swiftly downhill!

WRITTEN BY **CATHERINE CURZON**

Some marriages are made in heaven. Others, such as that of George, Prince of Wales, and his cousin, Caroline of Brunswick, are straight from hell. Far from being a romantic fairytale, when Caroline married the heir to the throne, it was the start of one of the most vitriolic royal tales that history has ever known.

Today we're used to our media-savvy royals gazing into one another's eyes, filled with hope for the future and dreams of a happy family, but in the Georgian era, love often didn't come into it. In the case of George and Caroline, the marriage was one of necessity. A compulsive spender with a love of women, George was drowning in debt. When he went cap in hand to his father, King George III, and begged for a handout, the monarch offered him a deal. If the prince would agree to marry Caroline, the daughter of the king's sister, then his debts would be settled. Caroline's family, meanwhile, accepted the suit readily. The princess had proven difficult to match with a prospective husband so to be offered the hand of the heir to one of the most powerful thrones in the world was an offer they couldn't and wouldn't turn down.

What the Prince of Wales didn't think to mention was the little fact that he was already married, having secretly wed Maria Fitzherbert, a Catholic widow, a decade earlier. Though that marriage was invalid under the terms of the Royal Marriages Act, Maria Fitzherbert considered it binding. Yet George knew that he had been checkmated and grudgingly said yes, he would marry Caroline of Brunswick. She was duly summoned to England and plans were laid for a glittering royal wedding. Upon arrival she found that her appointed lady-in-waiting was to be none other than Frances Villiers, the Countess of Jersey. Lady Jersey was a scheming and manipulative social climber. She was also the mistress of the Prince of Wales and, keen to stay in her lover's favour, was determined to report back on everything that Caroline said or did. There were, as was once said, three people in the marriage from the start.

The omens for the couple were terrible from the beginning. Upon arriving in London and meeting the prince, Caroline declared that he was far fatter

George, Prince of Wales

SOCIETY & SCANDAL

than his portraits and not half so handsome. For his part, George carped that Caroline's stench turned his stomach. At their very first meeting George demanded brandy to calm his horrified nerves then ran to the company of his mother. The public thought differently though, and as the family settled to a tense supper on the eve of the wedding, vast crowds gathered at the palace walls and called for the princess to give them a wave. This she did, much to the chagrin of her unpopular fiancé, who slammed the window to keep out the noise. It was an inauspicious start to a marriage of convenience that lurched from one scandalous disaster to another, and all of it in the full glare of the public spotlight.

It wasn't a blushing bridegroom who made his way to the altar of the Chapel Royal in St James's Palace on 8 April 1795. Instead, George was insensible with drink. The Prince of Wales was so paralytic throughout his wedding ceremony that his groomsmen had to physically drag him to the altar then hold onto him to keep him upright. He wept openly during the vows and tried to crawl from the chapel on his hands and knees as the Archbishop of Canterbury led the party in prayers. When the wedding night rolled around, it went as well as might be expected. Far from carrying his blushing bride over the threshold, George passed out in the thankfully empty fire grate. Caroline left him there and climbed into bed alone.

Though the Prince and Princess of Wales spent precious few nights together, the unfortunate couple somehow managed to have a child. Princess Charlotte of Wales, their only offspring, was born almost nine months to the day of their wedding. George, however, claimed that his bride was not only unhygienic, but far from virginal. Though he had dozens of lovers and she very likely had had none before her husband, George declared that he could never be intimate with her again or he would be left physically ill. For this royal couple, the concept of the heir and the spare was one that would remain unfulfilled.

The writing was on the wall for the newlyweds and within two years of that fateful ceremony in St James's Palace, the Prince and Princess of Wales were irretrievably estranged. For George, however, matters were typically complicated. Though he might hate Caroline, his father, George III, adored her. His own marriage to Charlotte, the prince's mother, was devoted and he had hoped that wedding bells might be all that were needed to set his eldest son on the straight and narrow. Seeing how George was treating Caroline, the king was incensed. His sympathies were all with the humiliated, dumped bride. George III knew too well of the prince's dissolute and immoral ways. He knew too of Maria Fitzherbert, having heard rumours regarding the entanglement even if he was never made aware of the wedding that had taken place all those years ago.

For George though, Mrs Fitzherbert was yesterday's news and whilst the Prince of Wales

When Caroline of Brunswick met the Prince of Wales on the eve of their wedding, she complained that he was nothing like his pretty portraits

went back to his womanising ways, Caroline set up residence across town. At her home in Blackheath she became a celebrated hostess, often entertaining the prince's most influential political foes. This drove George to distraction and he became convinced that she must be sleeping with the illustrious men who beat a path to her door, seeing this as the final humiliation. He did all he could to discredit Caroline, including accusing her of having an illegitimate child and subjecting her to a lengthy enquiry into her conduct, but Caroline continued to prevail. The so-called Delicate Investigation found that William Austin, the child George claimed was proof of his wife's infidelity, was in fact the son of a destitute couple. William's mother had come to Blackheath in search of work and Caroline had offered to take her son into her home and raise him with the best of everything. When William's parents appeared at the enquiry, the verdict became inevitable.

Far from providing proof that the wife of the heir to the throne had conceived a child with another man, all that the Delicate Investigation managed to prove was that Caroline was even more charitable and caring than had already

been known. By the investigation found her not guilty of adultery, the public had fallen for the queen of hearts. They loved Caroline and her celebrated philanthropy as much as they hated George, who was loathed for his largesse and shamelessly immoral ways, all of it funded by the hard-pressed taxpayer. William Austin, meanwhile, the little boy saved from poverty at Blackheath, became Caroline's faithful retainer until the day of her death.

Tired of her husband's spies and with her access to her only child restricted following the Delicate Investigation, Caroline came to believe that she would never be able to live the life she wanted if she remained in England. Though it meant leaving her daughter, Charlotte, behind, Caroline left Britain and travelled to Europe, stopping first in

"The Prince of Wales was so paralytic during his wedding that his groomsmen had to drag him to the altar"

QUEEN OF HEARTS

The trial of Queen Caroline created a national scandal and the press and public gleefully devoured stories of her carefree life on the continent

The Lost Princess

When the ill-fated couple's only child died, even that became a weapon for the Prince of Wales

According to the Prince of Wales he and his bride, Caroline of Brunswick, were intimate only three times. Nine months almost to the date of their wedding their only child, Princess Charlotte of Wales, was born. Charlotte was a bright and feisty young woman, who had a love of politics and drama, and the public adored her. Her marriage to Prince Leopold of Saxe-Coburg-Saalfeld was blissful but it was also short. Tragically, Charlotte died whilst delivering a stillborn child.

Across Britain, people grieved as they never had before. Haberdashers sold out of black cloth, schools and public buildings closed as a mark of respect and some shops feared bankruptcy as the country ground to a halt to mourn. Wracked by guilt, Sir Richard Croft, the respected doctor who had delivered Charlotte's stillborn son, later took his own life.

George, however, didn't think to tell Caroline that her only daughter was dead. She found out by accident, when a royal messenger on his way to deliver the news to the pope happened to stop off near her residence in Italy. It was the final straw for the embattled princess and she was determined to come back fighting against her estranged husband.

her homeland of Brunswick before she continued on her way. Once she was embarked on her continental travels Caroline really began to kick up her heels and there was nothing her furious husband could do about it. She travelled the continent and settled in Italy, where she took up with a former soldier named Bartolomeo Pergami. The Princess of Wales installed the dashing gentleman as her chamberlain and, if the rumours were to be believed, her lover too. The couple lived openly together with Pergami's young daughter and in the United Kingdom the people rejoiced at the knowledge that she was making a right royal fool of her husband.

Through all of this, George seethed and fretted. Though he had no shortage of lovers of his own, the knowledge that Caroline had managed to win not only the love of the people but also find personal happiness drove the capricious prince into a fury. He sent spies to Europe, intending to gather evidence of her adultery and secure a divorce once and for all. George's agents interviewed witnesses and servants and began to assemble a pile of circumstantial evidence, including rumours of shared beds, of the couple bathing together or trysting in sheltered carriages. They even reported back on whether the amount of urine in a bedroom chamberpot suggested that it had been used by one or two people overnight! The prince was certain that it was dynamite and when he had all the evidence he could muster, he delivered it to Parliament along with a request for a divorce.

What George hadn't reckoned with was the ill health of his ailing father. With his son reigning as Prince Regent since 1811, George III had been confined at Windsor for almost a decade. Blind, immobile and totally in the grip of his infamous madness, the old king died on 29 January 1820. Suddenly the Regent was catapulted onto the throne and for the newly-enshrined King George IV, nothing could be more embarrassing than his fun-loving wife, who was reported to dance without her stays and cavort in gowns that left nothing to the imagination. With time pressing and his coronation approaching, George was determined that she wouldn't be crowned as queen alongside him. More than anything, he needed to finalise that divorce.

Although Parliament offered Caroline a generous payment to stay in Europe and keep her head down, she had other ideas. Determined to face the House of Lords and the divorce proceedings that her husband had initiated, she headed for Britain and arrived to a hero's welcome. She was greeted by the Pains and Penalties Bill, an audacious scheme to put Caroline on trial for adultery. If she was found guilty, she would lose her title, her reputation would be in tatters and her marriage would be over. With his carefully gathered evidence, George was sure he couldn't lose.

Princess Charlotte of Wales

Non Mi Recordo

Being the star witness in a case of royal divorce isn't all fun and games

Of all the witnesses called for the prosecution, the star was undoubtedly Italian Theodore Majocchi. A servant in the household of Caroline of Brunswick and her rumoured lover, Bartolomeo Pergami, Majocchi's scandalous revelations of their affair were supposed to seal her fate. So shocked was Caroline to see her faithful servant take the stand that she gave an exclamation of fright and fled the House of Lords before he gave evidence against her.

Able to remember the smallest detail of the supposed affair when questioned by the prosecution, when defence counsel Brougham challenged him, Pergami's memory seemed to fail him. He answered every question with "non mi ricordo", or "I don't remember." So often did he use the phrase that eventually it became the subject of jokes, songs, poetry and caricature. Majocchi was nicknamed Signor Non Mi Ricordo by the media and everywhere he went, people called the phrase out after him.

Bruised and humiliated, Majocchi was one of many who learned that it wasn't wise to pit one's wits against those of Baron Brougham and Vaux.

Henry Brougham, 1st Baron Brougham and Vaux

Caroline's trial for adultery might have found her guilty but her feisty performance meant there would be no divorce from her husband

QUEEN OF HEARTS

"There were rumours of shared beds and baths. George's spies even reported back on the contents of the couple's chamberpots!"

Of course, just as he was in so many things, George was proved wrong. Ably defended by her skilful counsel, Henry Brougham, 1st Baron Brougham and Vaux, Caroline cut a confident figure before the Lords. Brougham savaged the witnesses for the prosecution and outside the walls of Westminster, the public couldn't get enough of the scandal. Newspapers reported daily on proceedings and printshops, balladeers and diarists fuelled the appetite for gossip. Far from being outraged to hear of Caroline's supposed fling with her chamberlain, the public loved it, and the princess became a rallying point for radicals and romantics alike. She was finally showing the dissolute George what it was like to be humiliated and as the trial limped along, he began to realise that he had made a terrible mistake.

In the event, however, the Lords found in favour of George by the narrowest majority imaginable and the bill was passed with a majority of just nine votes. Across the country the mood turned bitter and Lord Liverpool, the prime minister and no friend to Caroline, declared that the bill would not proceed to the Lords. There was to be no divorce for George IV and Caroline of Brunswick.

The delighted Caroline basked in her triumph. She was not only still married, she was now on the road to becoming queen and when the day of the Coronation came around, Caroline was at Westminster Abbey by dawn. She toured from door to door demanding admission but found them all barred to her on the express orders of the new king. Some of the doorkeepers jeered at Caroline's efforts and to add to the humiliation, so did the public who had for so long adored her. Never before had Caroline misjudged the mood of the country so badly as she did on that day in July 1821. The people who had gathered to watch the magnificent Coronation procession did so because they were ready to party. They no longer had any time for Caroline's drama and, just as they had built her up, now they tore her down.

Humiliated, Caroline retreated into seclusion in Brandenburg House and died within a few short weeks. King George IV was finally free of the woman he hated. Yet it was a pyrrhic victory, for the monarch's health was failing too. Decades of feasting and carousing had left him obese and sickly and he died less than a decade after his wife, as isolated at Windsor as his beloved father had been before him. For Caroline and George, the ill-fated cousins who became husband and wife, the price of marriage had been high indeed.

SOCIETY & SCANDAL

THE ORIGINAL PEOPLE'S PRINCESS

Nearly 200 years before Princess Diana, another princess symbolised the cult of celebrity, with both her short life and untimely death obsessed over by the press

WRITTEN BY **NELL DARBY**

Diana, Princess of Wales was commemorated after her premature death in 1997 as 'the People's Princess' – a woman with the common touch, who brought a touch of modernity to the royal family. After her death, there was a period of mass mourning that some said had never been seen on that scale before. Yet back in 1817, the death of another young princess had seen similar scenes of tears, mass mourning and melodramatic press coverage. Another Princess of Wales had died, and it was with her life – and death – that the cult of celebrity, particularly in relation to royalty, was really born.

Princess Charlotte Augusta had had an inauspicious start in life. Her father, Prince George of Wales (later the Prince Regent and King George IV), was unpopular with the British people. Rather than being quiet and statesmanlike, he enjoyed an extravagant lifestyle, spending a huge amount on his palaces, furnishings and parties. *The Times* described him as a man who "at all times would prefer a girl and a bottle to politics and a sermon." Taking on a mistress, the twice-widowed, Roman Catholic Maria Fitzherbert, in 1785, he secretly married her – despite the marriage being invalid, both because of Maria's religion and because George's father, George III, had not consented.

This relationship only ended – albeit temporarily – in 1794, when George announced his intention to marry his cousin, Caroline of Brunswick. This decision was not one made out of love, but because George had been promised more money if he agreed to it. George was dependent on an income from the government, but had been spending far more than he received. His marriage, then, was – on his part at least – one of convenience and greed.

George agreed to marry Caroline without having even met her and once they finally did meet, they instantly disliked one other. After their wedding ceremony on 8 April 1795, George got so drunk that he fell into his fireplace. Princess Charlotte, their only child, was born nine months after the marriage, but by the time of her birth, her parents had already separated.

It was into this toxic environment that Charlotte was born and grew up. Her father allowed her only limited contact with her mother, having specified in a will made when his daughter was just three days old that Caroline of Brunswick should play no part in Charlotte's upbringing. The young girl was therefore to be brought up largely by servants and governesses in the royal household. Yet Caroline remained defiant towards her estranged husband, and made 'secret' visits to, and carriage trips with, her daughter, knowing that the public would see them and that the press would report the trips. In this way, Charlotte became a pawn between her parents, and her mother's weapon.

22

THE ORIGINAL PEOPLE'S PRINCESS

With Princess Charlotte's death, the cult of royal celebrities was born

SOCIETY & SCANDAL

Caroline of Brunswick resorted to 'secret' meetings with Charlotte

Both the public and the press held a dislike for George IV

Although Caroline had been forbidden from playing a part in Charlotte's upbringing, the two shared a close relationship

O my dear Mama how happy your letter has made me; I hardly know which delights me most, to think you are come back safe, and well; or that I shall see you so soon. But I must tell you I fear I have the hooping cough, and I know not whether you have ever had it.

I am my dear Mama,

your ever Affte & Dutiful Daughter — Charlotte —

Despite her father's unpopularity with the British public, the birth of Charlotte was seen as a new start by the nation – she heralded new hope and the start of a modern royal family. It is no wonder that the press keenly followed her progress, reflecting its readership's interest in this young girl. It also reflected contemporary concern about George's attitude towards both her and her mother; in 1804, Cobbett's Weekly Political Register opined that if Charlotte remained under her father's control, she would become "contaminated," and sarcastically debated, "whether the amiable Princess of Wales or Mrs Fitzherbert is the most eligible preceptress of the infant Princess." In this way, it questioned whether Prince George was really the right person to "guard the religion and the virtue of his child," when he had been carrying on an affair with Maria Fitzherbert, and treating his wife – the mother of his child – so badly.

The guardianship of the young Princess was keenly discussed in the papers, as no doubt it was in the taverns and streets of both London and provincial areas. The expanding newspaper industry provided the public with information

THE ORIGINAL PEOPLE'S PRINCESS

The common touch

Did a shepherd really write a poem about Princess Charlotte?

Many of the poems written to commemorate Princess Charlotte's death were pastoral elegies. These were a form of poetry that was very popular at the time. But one poem written for Charlotte was particularly famous. It was apparently written, not by a well-known poet or an educated person, but by a more humble subject – a shepherd. This seems a bit too convenient, however. *The Carmen Pastorale; Or Pastoral Elegy On The Death Of HRH The Princess Charlotte Of Wales* clearly stated on its title page that it was "by a Shepherd" – but shepherds were often, at this time, illiterate.

If a shepherd really had produced such an elegy, he must have either had enough schooling to be able to write, to rhyme and to think of natural metaphors, and help at least in putting the oral version onto paper. And its relatively low cost – compared to other contemporary poems about the death, of between 1s 6d and 2s – suggests a desire to market it to less wealthy audiences, and thus to sell more.

Most of the poem is a conversation between two shepherds, Colin and Lubin, about "Clara," a "rosebud" who died before she had a chance to bloom. The setting is a hamlet, and Clara's death is the winter that follows a rural summer.

In stating that this poem was by a common man, making the scene-setting rural and featuring two shepherds, the publisher was cynically appealing to the ordinary people who had been won over by press depictions of this young, unstuffy royal, and to those who feared what the future of the royal family would now become. This was made explicit by the poem stating that as a result of Charlotte's death, "Albion [is] left to weep forlorn!/ Some foreign lord perchance may gain/ The birthright of her fair domain!"

In addition, though, such pastoral elegies of this time show there was a nostalgia here towards the rural past, as the industrial revolution gathered pace and threatened to change the face of Charlotte's, and the rural shepherd's, Britain.

An early 19th-century shepherd, in a typically pastoral scene

about the Princess, encouraged debate of controversial issues over her parenting, and turned Charlotte into a celebrity – any mention of her name was deemed newsworthy.

In 1809, the papers recorded that Princess Charlotte of Wales's birthday was celebrated on 7 January at Saint Julio's Cottage, Cheltenham. They also discussed many of the key attendees at a dance held to celebrate "the anniversary of the day that gave birth to this Illustrious Princess, so proudly and so justly the idol and future hope of her virtuous grandfather's true and loyal subjects." The dance was not attended by Charlotte, but instead organised by royalists who saw every reason to celebrate her birth. It is significant that her father was not mentioned in this report; Princess Charlotte was instead seen as George III's rightful heir, rather than her less popular father, George IV.

There was considerable interest in what the young Charlotte wore and what she did. When she attended her grandfather's birthday celebrations at Saint James's Palace in June 1807, the 11-year-old Princess was said to have worn "a pink and silver slip, with a beautiful Brussels lace frock to wear over it, and a pink and silver girdle." Then, six years later, it was reported that her birthday was celebrated at Cranbourn Lodge in Windsor, where her aunts visited in the morning and

> *"She refused to use the chair of the state saying, 'I prefer going up in the manner a seaman does'"*

presents were given before music was performed. Her private life – her skill at the piano, her love of music generally and her eager attendance at musical parties, together with visits to seaside resorts such as Weymouth in Dorset – was keenly observed and reported on.

Her unconventional upbringing – largely away from the royal household, where she spent time climbing trees and playing with boys – meant that she was perceived as more of a commoner, in some ways, than a royal. In 1815, while at the seaside, she had asked to go on board a 'very fine ship'. A bishop, standing near her, asked if she thought her father would approve, and Charlotte's response was that Elizabeth I had not been afraid to go on board a ship, so why should she? She then refused to use the chair of state provided to carry her into the ship, saying, "I prefer going up in the manner a seaman does." On another occasion, she had been walking in the grounds at Claremont, her house in Surrey, when she had bumped into one of the gardeners and started a conversation with him. When he said he did not own a Bible, she ran into the house and came back with one, which she inscribed with his name and the added statement: "From his friend, Charlotte."

In eagerly covering her words and her actions, the press created a celebrity out of Charlotte. They made sure their readers knew what Charlotte was doing, what she was wearing, how she spoke and who to. However, their depiction of her did not reflect her complexity; the stories about her were written to fit the image of her that the press wanted to create and promote – one of a royal with a 'common touch', who could bring the nation together. Similarly, paintings and engravings of her romanticised her, making her slimmer, darker haired and more beautiful than she actually was. Some of those who had met her stated how much she looked like her father, George; and that she had such pale skin and hair – including lashes and brows – that she looked almost colourless. However, this is not the image given by contemporary illustrations of her.

The press may have been on Charlotte's side, but this meant, conversely, it became increasingly critical towards Charlotte's father and the way he brought her up; she was very much their

25

SOCIETY & SCANDAL

William, Hereditary Prince of Orange, and later William II of the Netherlands, was George's choice for Charlotte's husband

Arranging a marriage
Charlotte's love life intrigued the press, but infuriated her father

Princess Charlotte proved that she had a mind of her own when it came to marriage. A priority of her father's, as well as the royal courtiers and politicians, was to see her make an advantageous match with a member of European royalty, and to produce an heir to the British throne. However, who her husband would be ultimately became a long battle of wills between Charlotte and Prince George.

George wanted her to marry William of Orange, the future king of the Netherlands, who was seen by others as ugly, thin, sallow and "spindle-legged." Charlotte initially agreed to this, but doubts rapidly grew after she found out that she was to be sent to live in the Netherlands for several months each year – she saw this as a sign that her father wanted to banish her from Britain. The engagement proved unpopular with the public, and with Charlotte, and she broke the engagement off in 1814. Despite George's anger, she proved recalcitrant. The breaking of the engagement was discussed in the House of Commons; one MP suggested that they should write to the Prince Regent, as he now was, to see if there was any likelihood of the marriage taking place, but it was decided that this motion was "most indiscreet, most indelicate, and most indecent." Rumours about the marriage – or lack thereof – were eagerly repeated in the newspapers. There were personal attacks on the Prince Regent, and the stories about him excluding Caroline from her daughter's life, and offering her money to do so, were brought up again as evidence of his cruelty and blame for Charlotte being encouraged to marry someone against her will.

Newspapers noted sympathetically that Charlotte did not want to marry the man her father approved of, only to regret it later in life, and "wisely asserted her own right to choose for herself in the most important action of her life."

Her choice of husband was Prince Leopold of Saxe-Coburg-Saalfeld – a man with little power, influence, money or territory, who was regarded as being somewhat unsophisticated. However, he had brains and a good temper, and the couple had a happy – if very brief – marriage.

heroine and he the villain. When rumours started to fly around that Charlotte had broken off her engagement to the Hereditary Prince of Orange, the *Chester Chronicle* dedicated a column to its own 'observations' of the situation, where it inadvertently showed what others were criticising – from the severity of George's communications with Charlotte, to the choice of advisors appointed for the Princess by her father. The newspaper tried to argue that the Prince was 'kind and most affectionate' towards his daughter, not cruel, as others had apparently been suggesting – but in doing so, it highlighted the criticisms, rather than muting them.

The public was thrilled when Charlotte was finally married, to Prince Leopold – who she had met at a dance – at Carlton House on 2 May 1816, and the marriage itself was the subject of many column inches. It was reported that when she was taken in an open carriage to family at Warwick House three days before, "crowds lined the roads, and everywhere she was greeted with hurrahs and the waving of hats and handkerchiefs." Celebrations were held around the country – one Bath establishment, for example, invited the local gentry to a French-style "grand public breakfast" featuring Sally Lunn buns, ices and every delicacy

> "Paintings romanticised her, making her slimmer, darker haired and more beautiful than she actually was"

THE ORIGINAL PEOPLE'S PRINCESS

After a failed first engagement, Charlotte eventually married Prince Leopold

Charlotte died at Claremont House on 2 November 1817

Leopold was said to have been overwhelmed by his wife's death, later writings claiming that, "it was as if he had lost his heart"

possible. Charlotte's wedding clothes were, of course, subject of discussion - she had worn a "long train of silver brocade falling behind her; gossamer draperies shining with diamonds and silver embroidery flooded about her."

Of course, once the marriage had taken place, speculation immediately started about when Charlotte would produce an heir to the throne. Sadly, she miscarried in 1816, but once she announced that she was pregnant again in 1817, the gossips resumed their speculation - this time about what sex the baby would be, resulting in bets being made in shops across Britain. Yet again, the stories about Charlotte from this time were romanticised and didn't reflect the reality; throughout her pregnancy, for example, she had a rather unladylike mutton-chop and a glass of port for lunch each day, and was said to become depressed when her midwife, Sir Richard Croft, ordered her to have a cup of tea and some bread and butter instead.

Princess Charlotte delivered a much-wanted son at 9pm on 5 November 1817 at Claremont, more than two weeks after he was believed to be due, and after three days of contractions. Tragically, however, he was stillborn; when Charlotte was told that he was dead, she said simply, "I am satisfied. God's will be done!" It was initially thought that his mother would recover from the birth, having got through the labour well. Soon, however, it became apparent that Charlotte herself was not going to do so - she started being sick and became progressively unwell, struggling to breathe. She died at 2am on 6 November, aged 21.

Her death, as detailed in depth in both provincial and national newspapers, was announced first to Lord Bathurst and the Duke of York. They then met at York House to discuss what to do, and sent a messenger to find George, Charlotte's father, at his home at Carlton House. He, however, had

SOCIETY & SCANDAL

Charlotte would marry Prince Leopold, Queen Victoria's uncle

been out that evening, and on travelling home, missed the messenger going the other way, having found the Prince away from home. The Prince sent a message to the Home Office to find out if Charlotte had had her baby; he got the response that she had been delivered of a dead son, but that she was "going on very favourably." When he was eventually told that his daughter was dead, it was reported that his state was "deplorable" – "the long looked-to sceptre of his father is miraculously broken upon the grave of his only child." There is some cynicism evident here as to whether the father was upset for the loss of a child, or the future king was upset for the loss of an heir.

Charlotte's husband, Leopold, meanwhile, remained at Claremont, where it was said he was as "composed as he could be in his broken-hearted state." However, later, he was regarded as being overwhelmed by the death, even following the wheel-tracks made by the carriage they travelled in when they had last gone out together. His state was made worse by the fact that Charlotte's body was embalmed, something he had apparently not expected to happen; when he went to the room where she lay in state, he sank to his knees in shock at her appearance in the coffin, looking as though she was simply sleeping.

The reaction of the press and public was similarly shocked and overwhelmed. It was noted

Englands ONLY H.
A Specimen of Conjugal affection & attention

THE ORIGINAL PEOPLE'S PRINCESS

that there was universal public grief, described as being "like a convulsion of nature." She was a "beloved female," held in high estimation; she had inspired the hopes of "all classes of people." This last point was particularly emphasised. Charlotte had been a Princess, but she had also "despised the forms and deceptions of her public station." She was "more like the head of a common family than the future mistress of a mighty empire." Those from even humble ranks in society therefore liked her, identified with her. They had particularly liked her continued devotion and respect for her mother, even as Caroline was persecuted by George. Many from the lower echelons of society marked her death by wearing black armbands, showing how devastated they were.

The grief was also because the two youngest generations of legitimate royals had been wiped out, and fears over the 'advanced age' of George's apparent inability to produce healthy and legitimate heirs meant that the House of Hanover's future looked very precarious. This resulted in a "frightful gloom upon the future destiny of the country itself," said one paper. Charlotte's death was not just mourned because a young woman had lost her life, but because it was seen as a herald of the death of the House of Hanover, and of the nation itself. Charlotte had been seen as a woman with enormous promise, who would have made a good Queen. One paper stated:

"If in her tender years she exhibited so much courage and resolution, what might we not expect when experience had cooled the impetuosity of the passions, and a knowledge of a free people enlightened her views of administration?"

Charlotte had represented the hopes of the people, and in her absence, all they had were much-criticised male members of the royal family. It would be another two years before a new female, legitimate, royal - Victoria - would be born, and with her the hopes of the nation rose again.

Charlotte's death also reflected the cult of celebrity, which had its origins in the 18th century, but which was really reaching its peak with the Romantic movement of this time. The early deaths of well-known individuals created a particular fame where the 'celebrity' became an object of enduring fascination despite, or because of, their demise. Charlotte was remembered not for any particular achievements - given that she was a 21-year-old woman in a patriarchal society, there was a limit to how much she could have achieved in her short life - but because she was young, attractive, royal and tragically dead. It was noted that immediately after her death, there was an increase in church congregations, with an increasingly secular society suddenly flocking to church to 'mourn' their Princess.

The cult of celebrity also ensured that Charlotte was commemorated in print culture both in Britain and overseas, from the newspaper obituaries to poetry. In France, poet Monsieur Surenne wrote:

O Heaven! What dreadful infliction of woe!
Our senses are stunn'd by the weight of the blow

While in England, Mary Cockle's elegy started:

A Kingdom mourns - a nation's sorrows flow;
And public anguish joins the private woe!
A star is set! That star whose cheering light,
Pierc'd the deep gloom of Britain's wintry night...

Surenne's poem showed that Charlotte's death had shocked in a way that death at an old age, or after a long illness, might have done. Cockle's poem focused on Charlotte's image as the herald of a new kind of royal. This emotional response to Charlotte's death - the death of a celebrity who the public felt they 'knew' - was, however, a response little different to the laying of flowers outside Kensington Palace in 1997.

The press and public fell in love with Charlotte, and they regularly covered what she was doing, what she was wearing and who she was with

LEFT Advice leaflet for pregnant women following Princess Charlotte's death

CENTRE This tragic deathbed scene by George Cruikshank shows how Charlotte's death in 1817 resulted in national grief at the loss of 'England's only Hope'

How to 'Make It' in Regency

LONDON

Our guide to surviving the social season in one piece

WRITTEN BY **JESSICA LEGGETT**

From 1811 to 1820, Prince George, the eldest son of King George III and Queen Charlotte, was appointed as Prince Regent of the United Kingdom on behalf of his father. The king, who had suffered from recurring bouts of mental illness and breakdowns, had been deemed unfit to rule. Although George's reign as Prince Regent lasted less than a decade, it was a time of great cultural, political and social change that subsequently became known as the Regency period.

When thinking of the Regency - or 19th century England in general - the social season probably crosses your mind. Coinciding with the sitting of Parliament, members of the upper class, known as 'the ton', would arrive in London from their stately, country homes to engage in both politics and socialising.

Although the timing of the season shifted, it typically started in January or February and ended in July or August and was a time for fashionable society gatherings, as well as the perfect opportunity to arrange marriages.

Surviving the social season revolved around many factors including etiquette, fashion and avoiding scandal - here's our guide on how to 'make it' among the highest echelon of British society.

SOCIETY & SCANDAL

DO'S & DON'TS
DO:
- Brush up on the rules of etiquette before heading to London
- Maintain formal behaviour even after you have been introduced to someone

DON'T:
- Give overt displays of emotion, unless you have to faint
- Meet with a gentleman without a chaperone present

MIND YOUR MANNERS
Etiquette was a high-stakes game

It was extremely important to be aware of the rules of etiquette before arriving in London for the social season. If you failed to meet the high standard of behaviour expected from members of the ton in their gatherings then your reputation would be at risk. This was especially a concern for the ladies, as a damaged reputation would hamper their marriage prospects and consequently their entire future.

To avoid making any embarrassing faux pas, many upper-class young ladies would prepare for the season by taking etiquette lessons. These lessons would include learning how to enter and leave a room; how to maintain a straight posture when sitting, standing and walking; and, of course, how to approach the queen and curtsy properly.

When it came to introductions, gentlemen were introduced to the ladies and not the other way round. A gentleman could not approach a lady without a formal introduction, and this could not occur until all parties agreed to be introduced. Remaining formal even after an introduction was a must and referring to another person by their first name (unless you were related) was a no-go.

Gentlemen were expected to be chivalrous while ladies had to be polite, elegant and calm, avoiding displays of obvious emotion, even when it came to laughing. However, while a lady had to be poised at all times, it was always appropriate for her to faint if faced with crude behaviour.

The biggest etiquette rule of them all was that a lady should never be alone in the company of a gentleman unless they were related or married to them, as this would attract gossip. If a lady did meet a gentleman a chaperone always had to be present. In fact, ladies were not supposed to go out alone at all and were always to be accompanied by another lady or servant – although this rule did relax towards the end of the Regency.

GET YOUR DANCING SHOES ON
A chance to make a good impression

No social season was complete without a dizzying array of balls to attend. The most important one was Queen Charlotte's Ball, where debutantes were formally presented to the court. Without attending the queen's ball, you could not join the marriage market.

Debutantes were typically between the ages of 16 and 18 when they were introduced to society. It was ideal for a lady with younger sisters to be married first before they were presented to society.

Balls and dances were supervised by a Master of Ceremony, who ensured that the event went smoothly, and who was responsible for formally introducing the young women and men.

Ladies would wear dance cards with a list of dances scheduled for the evening on their wrists. These cards helped them to keep track of the dances that they had promised to different partners – and potential suitors – throughout the night. However, a lady could not promise a dance until she was formally introduced to the gentleman in question.

Balls and dances gave ladies the perfect opportunity to meet several eligible gentlemen and vice versa. Yet a lady also had to take care not to dance with the same man more than twice – or, heaven forbid, all night – as this would attract gossip regarding the nature of their relationship and put her reputation at risk.

DO'S & DON'TS
DO:
- Attend Queen Charlotte's Ball to signal your entrance into high society
- Fill your dance card and get to know your potential suitors

DON'T:
- Promise a dance without being formally introduced
- Dance with the same gentleman more than twice in one night

REGENCY LONDON

DRESS TO IMPRESS
Keeping up with the latest fashion trends was a must

Ladies and gentlemen wishing to get through the season needed to ensure that their wardrobe was up to scratch unless they wanted to become social pariahs. Regency dresses were characterised by a raised, empire waistline and a narrow, ankle-length loose skirt. During the day, ladies were not to expose their chest or arms, and so their dresses would have long sleeves with a tucker or chemisette to cover the chest. They were supposed to wear bonnets if they were out in the daytime, and a lady always had to wear her hair up once she was formally out in society.

Meanwhile, it was acceptable to wear short sleeves and lower necklines in the evening, although ladies had to wear elbow-length white or light-coloured gloves made from leather or cotton. Dresses were made from sumptuous fabrics such as satin and they were decorated - albeit sparingly - with intricate embroidery.

For Queen Charlotte's Ball, debutantes had to wear a white court dress and a headdress decorated with ostrich feathers. The queen insisted on retaining the wide-hooped skirts, popular in the late 18th century, for court dress even though they had fallen out of fashion. These dresses also had a shortened bodice in line with Regency fashion and so the wide skirt began at the waistline under the bust. This resulted in a unique silhouette. The requirement for wide-hooped skirts finally ended when the Prince Regent ascended the throne as King George IV in 1820.

As for gentlemen, it was common for them to wear breeches during the early years of the Regency. They eventually moved on to long trousers or fitted pantaloons, worn with Hessian or two-toned top boots. White linen shirts with a straight, upright collar were a must, finished off with a cravat. Men would also wear a tall top hat when out during the day. Many men took their lead from Beau Brummell, the society figure and close friend of the Prince Regent, who set the leading trends for men's clothing.

DO'S & DON'TS
DO:
- Wear a bonnet or hat when you are out and about for the day
- Adhere to the rules of court dress for Queen Charlotte's Ball

DON'T:
- Expose your arms or chest in the daytime if you are a lady
- Get caught wearing old-fashioned trends

DO'S & DON'TS
DO:
- Try to marry a wealthy bachelor
- Find a bride that has a sizeable dowry

DON'T:
- Marry a lady who is below your station
- Forget that love is also a desirable factor for marriage

MEET YOUR MATCH
Finding a spouse was the name of the game

To think of marriage among the upper classes in Regency England probably conjures up images of bossy mothers foisting their daughters on prospective suitors at every opportunity - and this isn't entirely wrong. Once young ladies had been officially introduced into society they needed to secure a suitable husband by joining the marriage market, the throng of single ladies and gentleman looking for a spouse.

Finding the right husband or wife involved many factors. Marriage offered an opportunity to climb the social ladder and form or strengthen family alliances, so marrying below one's station was not ideal, especially for gentlemen. If a lady did marry someone who was of a higher social status, not only would her status rise but so would her family's by virtue. Also, if the eldest daughter made a good marriage, it gave her sisters who were due to join the marriage market a better chance too.

Wealth was also an important factor because daughters, unlike sons, did not inherit their father's estate and so their financial security often depended on their future spouse. A good dowry boosted a lady's prospects and securing a wealthy husband also meant that she would have the means to take care of her family if needed. For gentlemen, marriage was all about producing an heir to secure his family line and finding a wife who was capable of managing the household.

Although there was a lot of pressure to find a good match in terms of wealth and social status, love was not always out of the question. If couples were desperate to be together but their parents disapproved, they always had the option of eloping to Scotland, where the law on marriage was not as restrictive. In particular, the Scottish village of Gretna Green became a popular destination for elopements.

33

SOCIETY & SCANDAL

GET OUT AND ABOUT Becoming the social butterfly of the season

There were a variety of activities to keep the ton entertained while in London for the season, such as card parties, museums, horse races, dinner parties, rides in the park, and the theatre. The more you were out and about, the more opportunities you had to socialise with others.

A classic season activity was to go promenading - a leisurely walk in a public place - allowing you to see and been seen by other members of high society. Courting couples would often promenade together, always in the presence of a chaperone, to show off their relationship.

Ladies and gentleman would also find themselves clamouring to be accepted into a range of exclusive social clubs in the city. The most famous and exclusive of them all was Almack's Assembly Rooms, also known as 'the Marriage Mart', where gentlemen would look for a suitable bride.

Almack's was run by the Lady Patronesses, the six or seven most influential ladies of the ton. These ladies decided who could be admitted into Almack's to attend the club's weekly ball and you could only purchase a voucher with their permission. This voucher could also be taken away by the Patronesses if they deemed you were not worthy after all, something that amounted to social disaster.

Their control over the club did not sit well with everyone, with Captain Gronow, a Welsh Grenadier Guards officer and writer, claiming "the female government of Almack's was a pure despotism and subject to all the caprices of despotic rule".

Another popular place to go was London's public pleasure gardens, such as the iconic Vauxhall Gardens. Visited by people from all social classes, these pleasure gardens hosted concerts, masquerades, costume balls, fireworks, amusement rides and even zoos - some even offered hot air balloon rides. However, under the cover of darkness the gardens also offered an opportunity for couples to mingle without a chaperone or even sneak off, something that would cause a huge scandal if they were caught.

DO'S & DON'TS
DO:
- Be seen by other members of the ton
- Get yourself a voucher for the exclusive Almack's Assembly Rooms

DON'T:
- Cross the Lady Patronesses unless you want to be ostracised from society
- Get caught having an illicit meeting with your lover

AVOID THE GOSSIP PAGES Endangering your reputation could mean game over

One of the biggest objectives of making it through the social season was to come out unscathed by scandal or gossip. For ladies especially, anything that had the potential to negatively affect their reputation could prevent them from securing that all-important match with a prized suitor.

Reputation was so important that a gentleman could challenge another to a duel if they felt their reputation - or that of a lady's - had been slighted, to restore their honour. Duels were potentially deadly and illegal, so they typically took place at dawn so that the men were less likely to be caught.

It was during the Regency era that the steam-powered rotary press arrived, first adopted by *The Times* newspaper in 1814, making papers quicker and easier to print than ever before. Various newspaper columns and periodicals would be filled with pieces of salacious gossip, from affairs and elopements to gambling and hedonistic behaviour - often obtained from sources like servants or other ton members.

One such gossip column was the *Tête-à-Tête* in *Town and Country Magazine*, which predated the Regency as it folded in 1796, but had reported on illicit meetings between members of the elite. Although the people involved in the scandals were not explicitly named, their initials would be included and this - coupled with plenty of hints - would be enough for many readers to guess their identity. Sordid stories from the press would be shared over gambling tables, at Almack's and in coffeehouses, so it was not long before scandals among the ton became wider knowledge. Gossip also spread thanks to the popularity of caricatures of the elite.

Even members of the royal family could not escape the papers. The Prince Regent's brother, the Duke of York, found himself embroiled in a huge scandal when it was discovered that his mistress, Mary Anne Clark, had been illegally selling military commissions and promotions, reportedly with his knowledge. As Commander-in-Chief of the army, the duke faced a parliamentary inquiry and although he was cleared, his love letters to Mary were widely published in the press. Consequently, he was forced out from his position, but he was eventually reinstated.

DO'S & DON'TS
DO:
- Avoid indulging in disreputable behaviour that can land you in hot water
- Keep up to date with the latest gossip of the ton

DON'T:
- Insult or make a slur against someone else, unless you want to end up in a duel
- Let your guard down, because you don't know who is whispering stories about you to the press

George III, Queen Charlotte and their six eldest children, in a 1770 portrait by Johan Zoffany

BEHIND THE GLITZ AND GLAMOUR

Historian Catherine Curzon tells us what the social season was really like

What was it really like for the young women searching for eligible husbands in the marriage market? Was it as glamorous and exciting as period dramas would like to have us believe?
It was hard work! The jewel in the London social season was Queen Charlotte's Ball, where debutantes were presented to the queen. From that moment on, the girls were under intense pressure to secure a highly prized bachelor in their first season. If they didn't, their chances at a good marriage next year plummeted.

How costly was it for upper-class families to keep up with the fashions of high society?
It was enormously expensive. But it was vital for families to make it clear that they were rich enough to keep up - a bride needed a dowry and the bigger, the better. To put the figures in perspective, Mr Darcy's much-vaunted £10,000 per year would be worth millions today.

How influential were scandal sheets? Did they really have the power to seriously damage someone's reputation?
Though scandal sheets came later, there was plenty of gossip in the Regency press and readers lapped it up. Though scandal could destroy a reputation, for those willing to embrace their notoriety it could lead to fame and sometimes even fortune.

Was it possible for women to remain unmarried and support themselves with independent careers during the Regency period?
It was possible, but not common. Bluestocking Elizabeth Carter became renowned as a classicist and translator, while Anne 'Gentleman Jack' Lister famously controlled a portfolio of business interests that included mining, agriculture and quarrying, as well as presiding over Shibden Hall with her wife, Ann Walker.

In your opinion, what is one of the biggest misconceptions about the Regency social season and the other cultural practices around it?
While it's commonly believed that love had no part in the marriage market, that wasn't always the case. After all, Princess Charlotte of Wales refused to marry the husband chosen for her by her father, the Prince Regent. Instead she stood her ground and married for love to a prince who had plenty of pedigree, but precious little money.

The Scandal of George III's Court *by Catherine Curzon is out now from Pen & Sword*

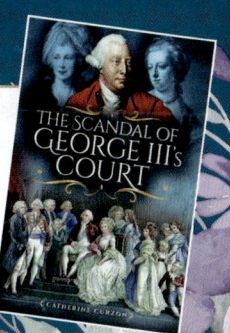

SOCIETY & SCANDAL

Luke Newton and Ruby Barker as Colin Bridgerton and Marina Thompson in the 2020 Netflix television adaptation *Bridgerton*, whose elopement was thwarted by Lady Whistledown

RUNNING AWAY TO
GRETNA GREEN

Why did Regency Britain see such a boom in elopements and what was the lure of Gretna Green?

WRITTEN BY **EMMA SLATTERY WILLIAMS**

"It is a truth universally acknowledged, that a single man in possession of a good fortune, must be in want of a wife" – these immortal, yet ironic, words opening Jane Austen's 1813 novel *Pride and Prejudice*, highlight the central role matrimony played during the Regency period. Parents were desperate to ensure their children made a good match – for daughters this was about survival, for sons it was about producing an heir and a financial union between families. Marriages were arranged with little input from the betrothed, so is it any surprise couples defied convention and fled to Gretna Green?

In 1754, the Clandestine Marriages Act (known as Lord Hardwicke's Marriage Act) came into force in England and Wales. The Act stipulated that a legally binding marriage must take place in a Church of England church, be conducted by a minister and those under 21 must have parental permission. It was also necessary for banns to be read at church three times.

Previously, anyone could marry provided an ordained vicar was present. This allowed for underage marriages, bigamy and secret matches without parental consent – and crucially this new law didn't apply in Scotland.

RUNNING AWAY TO GRETNA GREEN

Julia Sawalha and Adrian Lukis as Lydia Bennet and George Wickham in the 1995 BBC television adaptation of *Pride and Prejudice*, who ran away together to the horror of her family, before being saved from ruin by Mr Darcy

A 1798 cartoon by German artist Heinrich Joseph Schütz showing an officer smuggling his beloved out of her home to whisk her away to Gretna Green

"Elopements could be a desperate measure for loved-up couples, and a necessity if the woman was pregnant"

A 1785 cartoon by Georgian artist Thomas Rowlandson depicting a runaway couple on their way to Gretna Green being pursued by her father

To circumvent the new law, couples simply began eloping to towns on the Anglo-Scottish border. The romantic allure of places such as Gretna Green were first established in the 1770s, when a new toll road made Gretna one of the first easily accessible villages over the border. The only stipulations were that the bride must be over 12 and the groom 14. Under Scottish law, as long as vows were made in front of two witnesses the marriage was valid, with blacksmiths becoming popular 'anvil priests'.

Elopements could be a desperate measure for loved-up couples prevented from marrying, but also a necessity if the woman was pregnant – as was the motivation for *Bridgerton's* Marina Thompson's near elopement with Colin Bridgerton before scandal erupted. Some couples also chose covert marriages as they were far cheaper without the need of a marriage licence.

In 1812, Harriet Cholmondeley, illegitimate daughter of the Marquess of Cholmondeley, ran away to Gretna Green with an army officer. Both families opposed the match but later relented as an Anglican ceremony was held a few weeks later on her father's estate.

Runaway marriages captured the public's imagination and infiltrated popular culture – such as Lydia Bennet's elopement with the charming George Wickham in *Pride and Prejudice*. She leaves a note stating their intention to marry at Gretna Green, but Wickham had no such plans. Before scandal tarnishes the family, Mr Darcy intervenes to ensure they marry.

Once the dust had settled families could forgive an elopement as soon as a legal marriage took place but the couples still risked estrangement from their loved ones. When Sarah Child, heir to her banker father's fortune, ran away to Gretna Green with the Earl of Westmorland, her furious father pursued them, eventually shooting at their horse before they managed to escape and marry. He eventually had his revenge by entailing his fortune on his granddaughters rather than his grandson, the next Earl of Westmorland.

Less romantic motives sometimes led unscrupulous individuals to exploit these legal loopholes. Edward Gibbon Wakefield abducted 15-year-old heiress Ellen Turner in 1826, deceiving her into marrying him under the false pretence of saving her father from ruin. After their marriage in Gretna Green was discovered, it was swiftly annulled, and Wakefield sentenced to three years in prison for abduction.

SOCIETY & SCANDAL

REGENCY STYLE

REGENCY *Style*

Unravel the real-life fashions of the era

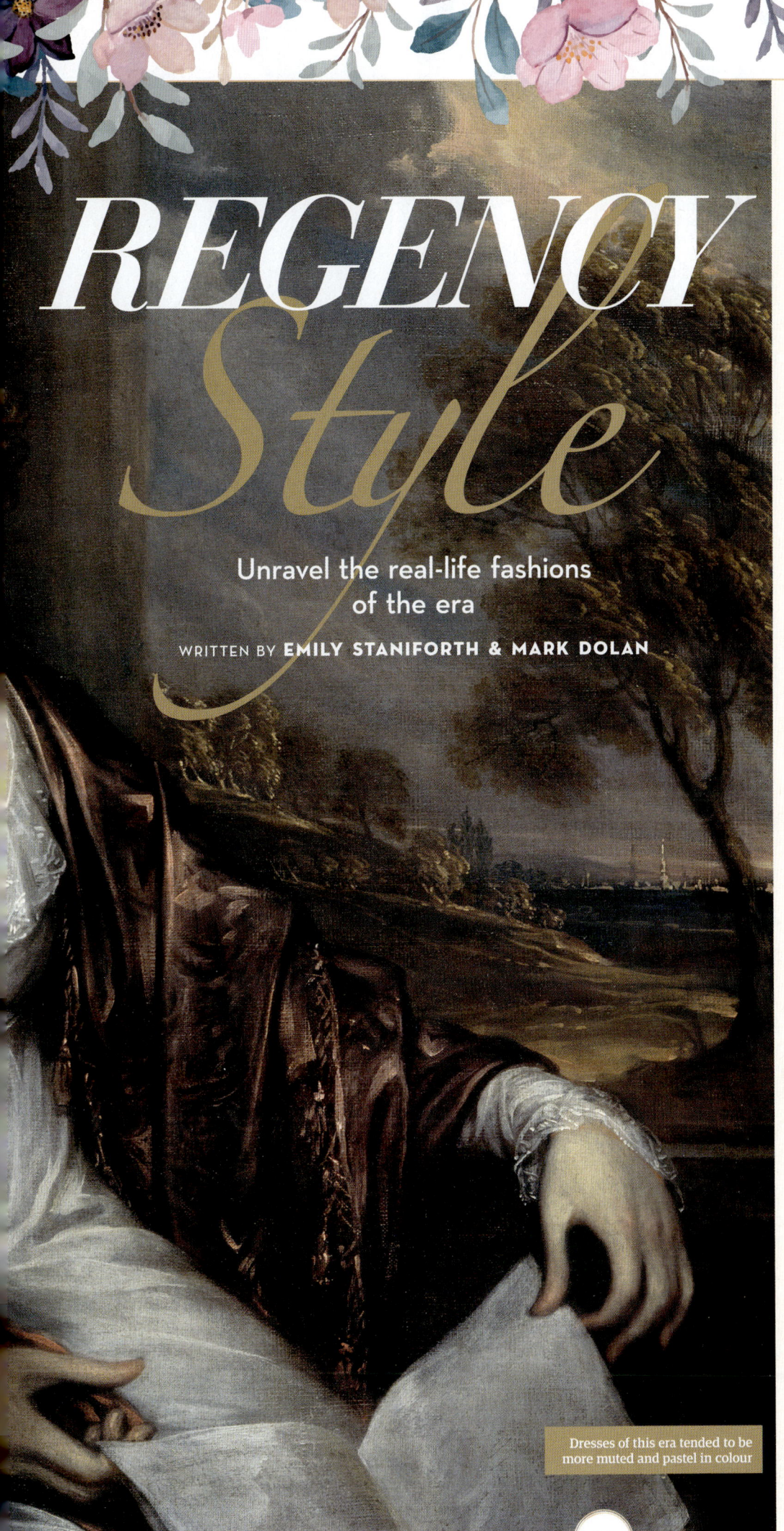

WRITTEN BY **EMILY STANIFORTH & MARK DOLAN**

The elegant and iconic fashion of the Regency era continues to capture the imagination of people today, largely due to the popularity of novels set in the period – such as those by Jane Austen or Julia Quinn – and the screen adaptations that bring Regency clothing to life. But how close are these outfits to the real-life attire of Regency women and men? At the dawn of the Regency period, a fresh style was emerging among the women and men of Europe. A new style for a new era, Regency fashion moved away from the trends that had come immediately before it, while still taking inspiration from the ancient past.

EVERYDAY DRESSING

After the voluminous fashionable skirts of the previous centuries, women's clothes became more muted in every aspect in the 19th century. Everything became smaller and more refined: dresses, headwear and accessories were understated compared to the extravagance that had come before. Skirts remained loose fitting, but instead of being expanded using undergowns and structured base layers, material draped downwards, skimming the body to create a new fashionable silhouette. This shape is now known as the 'empire line', but dresses of this silhouette were not named this until the 20th century.

Empire dresses first became fashionable in France where, after the Revolution (1789-99), people wanted to dress as differently as possible to the opulent and exaggerated style of the French aristocrats of the 18th century. This led to the development of the empire-style dress, which was fitted above the waist, retaining the low neckline that was fashionable in the previous century, but adapting it to make the cut less wide and obvious. Everything about the empire dress was softer and more delicate. The material was cinched under the bodice-covered bust, giving the illusion of a high waist and long legs, while the bottom of the garment flowed downwards and grazed the floor. This elegant new style was soon adopted by women across Europe, who not only took their inspiration from the new French trends, but also from the classical worlds of Ancient Greece and Rome. A renewed interest in these ancient societies saw women (and men) wanting to replicate the fashions they saw in art and sculpture, and the empire style closely resembled the flowing togas of the Romans and Greeks.

COLOURS AND MATERIALS

Once again rejecting previous trends, European women in the 19th century turned to a more pastel colour scheme when dressing themselves for day-to-day life. Gone were the days of deep reds, golds and purples, and instead whites, blues, lilacs, greens and pinks became all the rage. Dyes were expensive and so many of these colours were pale in tone. Furthermore, these dyes were not as vibrant as the aniline dyes that were discovered

Dresses of this era tended to be more muted and pastel in colour

SOCIETY & SCANDAL

Neoclassicism and Fashion

How fashionable young men took their leads from the ancient past

It is difficult to overstate the impact that Ancient Greece and Rome had on 19th-century European design. The Neoclassical movement was sparked by the work of a few key individuals, such as James 'Athenian' Stuart and Johann Joachim Winckelmann. Stuart was an artist who travelled to Italy in order to improve his painting skills and ended up studying and adoring the works of Ancient Greece and Rome. His book, Antiquities of Athens (1762), was the first accurate work on Classical Greek architecture and was hugely influential for architects and designers throughout Europe.

Winckelmann, an archaeologist and art historian, was similarly enamoured by the artistry of Ancient Greece and Rome, and extolled the beauty and perfection of its paintings and sculptures in his seminal work, Reflections on the Painting and Sculpture of the Greeks in 1765. In particular, he singled out the 'Apollo Belvedere' statue as a perfect example of the Greek mastery of form and the idealised male body. As interest in the ancient world grew, and new discoveries of ancient art were being unearthed, there flourished an appetite for visiting sites such as Rome, Pompeii and Athens (Lord Byron, on his Grand Tour, inscribed his name into the wall of the Temple of Poseidon at Sounion!) and collecting ancient artefacts among the upper classes.

Together, all of this fed into a fascination with the aesthetics of the Classical civilisations, which played a major role in the ideals of men's fashion espoused by the likes of Beau Brummell, with his focus on form-fitting clothing and the simple elegance that was epitomised by Greek and Roman art.

Young men's interest in Classical Greece fed into the fashion of the time, leading to form-fitting clothing

Regency period author, Jane Austen, is pictured here wearing an empire gown with an unusual high neckline and a bonnet

in the Victorian era, and so the vibrancy of the natural dyes used to colour Regency dresses faded as time wore on.

Towards the end of the 18th century, when the new French fashions were starting to take hold across the rest of Europe, women's dresses were made out of materials like cotton and wool. However, as time progressed and styles developed, more delicate fabrics began to be used. Silk and translucent cottons like muslin enabled women to emulate the classical fashions they aspired to, and created a more subtle and light appearance.

SILHOUETTES, STAYS AND STYLES

To create the desired empire silhouette, women commonly relied on a stay. Like a corset, a stay helped to mould a woman's body into the fashionable shape of the day. Instead of minimising the waist, it pushed the bust up to draw attention to a woman's chest: for women of the Regency period, the bustier a dress the better.

The female silhouette in the Regency era came courtesy of a stay, which pushed the bust up

REGENCY STYLE

EVENING WEAR

During the Regency period, women in the higher ranks of society commonly wore different outfits for different activities, all of which varied slightly depending on their purpose. A dress for staying at home, for example, would be similar to a dress worn to go promenading in the afternoon. Popular overcoats, like spencers and pelisses, may also have been worn for outdoor activities in the day. Dresses worn during the day were simpler in style and more practical, whereas in the evening, a fancier garment was worn to social occasions and engagements like balls, where the fanciest dresses of all were worn. Unlike the muslin and cotton fabrics worn during the day, evening dresses were made from richer and thicker silks and satins. However, this was the major difference between evening and daytime dress, with the styles for both purposes remaining fairly similar.

Empress Joséphine is painted here wearing a typical empire-style dress with decorated sleeves

Embroidery and lace or velvet trimmings were used to adorn what was an otherwise simple dress

> "Regency dresses, though more plain and simple than the fashion that had come before, were still ornately decorated"

The stay came in two forms depending on what a woman wanted to achieve for her body type. Short stays only went slightly below the breasts and were used primarily to accentuate the bust. Long stays, however, were worn by women who perhaps needed extra support in the chest area, or who wanted to smooth down their curves and appear slimmer in their dresses.

Regency dresses, though more plain and simple than the fashion that had come before, were still ornately decorated. Embroidery was the main way that garments were adorned, sometimes in a Grecian style. However, some women drew inspiration from military uniforms and trimmed their dresses with velvet or braiding. Others looked to fashion icons of the time, the most prominent of which was Napoleon Bonaparte's wife, Joséphine. Her love for silk dresses led more women to turn to the soft and luxurious fabric. She was also partial to ribbon and lace trimmings, which then became a popular form of decoration. Gifts from her husband's trips to Egypt enabled Joséphine to adorn her dresses with eastern patterns, which served as further inspiration to the women who admired her style.

From around 1810, Regency dresses started to become even more elaborate in their design and decoration, though nothing like the dresses fashionable in the late Renaissance. Retaining the high waistlines, the upper bodice became more structured while skirts incorporated elements of lace, slashing, tiering and ruffles. It wasn't until around 1825 that the waistlines of dresses started to drop back downwards.

SOCIETY & SCANDAL

Adaptations of Regency-period literature, such as the BBC's adaptation of Pride and Prejudice in 1995, reignites modern interest in the era's fashion

Beau Brummell was a trailblazer when it came to defining men's fashion in the Regency period

Empire-style dresses remained en vogue, and trains attached to the backs of these dresses became a fashionable option for an evening dress. However, these outfits had to be suitable for dancing in and therefore were not too long or cumbersome. Longer, earlier dresses sometimes had to be pinned up to enable a woman to participate in ball dances without worrying about tripping. Between the late 1790s and the 1820s, elaborate decorative ball dresses went in and out of style, with lace, feather and velvet embellishments dropping in and out of fashion.

RISE OF THE DANDY

Just like with womenswear, menswear was influenced by the French Revolution, which split fashion along two axes: time and gender. Firstly, gone were the frills, lace, colours, luxurious fabrics and intricate patterns of 18th-century men's clothing, and in were dark colours, simple fabrics – particularly wool – and plain, unadorned designs. Secondly, where previously both men and women had unity in a love of bright colours, complex shapes and silhouettes, and intricate decoration, all this fashionable playfulness, all the creativity, all the expansiveness, was left solely to women. Men now rejected such alleged frivolities in favour of the sober utilitarianism that embodied revolutionary ideals.

BEAU BRUMMELL

There is no single figure who embodied these new fashionable ideals and had more influence on menswear in the Regency period than George Bryan 'Beau' Brummell. Educated at Eton, he was presented to the then-Prince Regent, latterly King George IV, and the pair became fast friends. This was to be a very significant relationship for the burgeoning dandy, as it gave him a path into society, where he would make his mark.

Brummell's signature look, which once established he never reneged on, rejected the bright colours and elaborate ornamentation of the previous century. He kept to a colour palette of blue-black, white and buff, along with fitted silhouettes that showed off the figure rather than augmented or obscured it. The product of Brummell's tastes, preferences, rejections of convention, and influences was the precursor

REGENCY STYLE

Evening attire worn for balls did not differ too much from a woman's everyday wear

to the modern suit, ie a plain white shirt, dark coat and full-length trousers, finished off with an intricately tied cravat.

It was Brummell's life that shaped his style; his pared-back colour palette, for instance, was taken almost directly from the colours of Eton College, where he first began to become interested in clothing. After he joined the army, Brummell was required to purchase a uniform for his life in the 10th Light Dragoons, which included two garments that would go on to become his style staples: a blue coat and white trousers. His later fashion choices would also often incorporate the type of material used for the 10th's uniform, while his adherence to tight light-coloured trousers can be directly traced back to his time as one of the 'Prince's Own'.

With the growing interest in the art and culture of Ancient Greece and Rome, there are numerous references made by Brummell's contemporaries to his body, which naturally conformed to the proportions seen as representing the Greek ideal. His physicality, combined with the taste for Neoclassicism, allowed him to develop a style that utilised tight, form-fitting clothing to show off and flatter his silhouette rather than obscuring it. The coats he wore were an extension of this; being the most sculptural garments in his outfit, they offered London's tailors the chance to create a shape that did not simply mould to the wearer but gave the impression of classical nudity through the use of well-cut fabric and clean, sharp lines.

Taking their cue from Brummell, fashionable young Regency men often wore tight full-length pantaloons, favoured by Brummell, and commonly combined them with a knee-high boot, with turned-down tops and occasionally tassels – one of the few remaining flourishes that harked back to the pre-Revolution days – which were equally as tight, flaunting men's calves and adding a military air to civilian dress.

THE END OF REGENCY FASHION

By the end of the Regency era and beyond, silhouettes for men and women started to become more voluminous. For example, men's coats were broader at the shoulders and fuller at the chest, while trousers became wider. Even the cravat, a Regency staple, was supplanted by neckties. Womenswear saw a return of the larger skirt and a stop to straighter, flowy dresses that had once dominated. For some, like Queen Charlotte, large dresses and hooped underskirts had never gone out of style, but for many, they had to give up on their empire-style dresses in order to keep up with ever-changing fashions. By the time the Victorian era (1837-1901) was in full swing, the plainer, elegant Regency fashions were a distant memory.

"Regency With a Twist"

How do Netflix's *Bridgerton* outfits compare to real Regency fashion?

The clothing of the Regency era is a familiar sight in film and television, particularly in the acclaimed adaptations of novels by Jane Austen, such as *Pride and Prejudice* or *Emma*. But Regency fashion has become once more a topic of conversation in recent years due to the explosion in popularity of the *Bridgerton* series on Netflix. In the series, many of the female characters are dressed in the traditional and popular empire silhouettes that have become so synonymous with the Regency era, and the low necklines and accentuated busts featured on the show are also typical of the historical period.

The show's creator, Chris Van Dusen, is quoted as saying: "Everything is rooted in Regency times, but the volume is turned up… One example of that is that *Bridgerton* is a bonnet-free world. Our ladies wear hats, but they don't wear more traditional bonnets." The colours worn by the show's female characters are also much brighter than those that would probably have been worn in real life, with many colours having been chosen to reflect a character's personality.

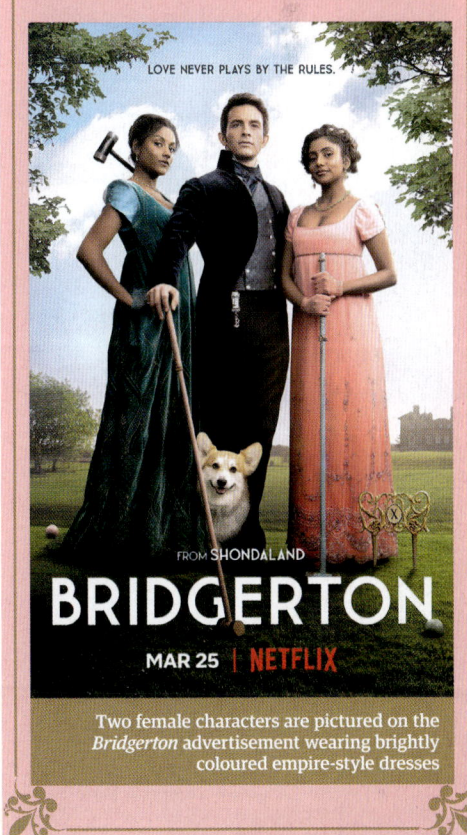

Two female characters are pictured on the Bridgerton advertisement wearing brightly coloured empire-style dresses

SOCIETY & SCANDAL

SCANDAL,
SATIRE AND THE PRESS

Uncover the rise of the press and tabloids in the Regency era

WRITTEN BY **MARK DOLAN**

Humans have always been held in thrall by gossip and scandal. It has even been suggested that gossip played a pivotal role in the development of early humans, with gossip allowing for the creation of social groups - an 'us' and a 'them'. The Regency and, indeed, the whole Georgian period, could be called the Golden Age of Gossip, with newspapers, scandal sheets, satirical cartoons and even novels all contributing to the intricate world of hearsay and speculation.

Newspapers first became the beating heart of the middle and upper classes at the very start of the 18th century, just over 100 years before the Regency era. *The Daily Courant* appeared for the first time in 1702, published by the printer and bookseller, Elizabeth Mallet. This newspaper, consisting of just one leaf, with news on the front and later advertisements on the back, was Britain's first daily newspaper. Although it initially focused only on foreign news, and purported to provide no comment on goings-on, the frequency with which it was published was revolutionary, and Mallet's influence can be felt throughout the next hundred years of British journalism.

It was not long before other printers saw the genius in Mallet's new schedule, and newspapers and magazines began popping up across London. One notable publication, which debuted in 1709, had a clear focus on gossip: *The Tatler*. The very first issue, appearing on 12 April, told of a young nobleman who fell in love with a woman he'd seen while he was brushing his teeth on his 21st birthday; he subsequently spent four years going mad trying to find her. A direct competitor soon sprang up. *The Female Tatler* also appeared for the first time in 1709, printed three days a week, each day when there wasn't an edition of *The Tatler*. It was written by a 'Mrs Crackenthorpe', a pseudonymous author described on the paper as "a Lady who knows every thing". Similarly to the fictional Lady Whistledown in *Bridgerton*, Mrs Crackenthorpe would take aim at known figures (contrary to Whistledown, targets weren't named, but they were made identifiable for those in the know) and attempt to educate young ladies on proper etiquette and behaviour in fashionable society. Although it lasted just one year (in that time there were over 100 editions!), *The Female Tatler* is notable for being not just written by a woman, but aimed at a female audience.

Newspapers continued to proliferate in the early years of the 18th century, and by 1712 there were 20 new papers in London alone. This increased competition led the printers to focus on being more attractive to the public than their rivals, and scandalous gossip was one of the best ways to hook potential readers. While many of these newspapers would include gossip about politicians and other members of the upper classes - those

The front page of a 1702 edition of The Daily Courant, Britain's first daily newspaper

SCANDAL, SATIRE AND THE PRESS

Lady Blessington, one of the most successful writers of fashionable novels in the early 19th century

SOCIETY & SCANDAL

whose lives held the most intrigue for the masses (the nascent 'celebrities' of the time) - others might discuss aspects of crime and punishment, including public hangings. True crime is no new phenomenon either!

Gossip columns became increasingly a core part of the social and political world of the upper and middle classes in Britain. It was not only the daily newspapers dedicating inches to the deeds and misdeeds of high society; weekly and monthly publications, such as *The World*, *The Connoisseur* and *The Lady's Magazine*, also made sure to include gossip columns.

Perhaps the most important periodical in the development of gossip columns was *Town and Country* magazine (no relation to the American magazine of the same name). While other magazines' articles would feature society news and some tales of scandal, *Town and Country* had the first true gossip column, 'Tête-á-Tête'. Each month, the writers would focus on a particular society couple - no names were mentioned but there were plenty of heavy hints as to their identities - to be profiled and have their love lives and scandals exposed and unpicked. This provided excellent fodder for people to discuss and digest in the coffeehouses and taverns.

It was not just newspapers or magazines that were the domain of scandal and gossip, however. One of the biggest media for satire and scandalous gossip in the Regency period was the caricature or satirical print. As with the birth of the daily newspaper, we have a woman to thank for the flourishing of the Golden Age of Caricature: Mary Darly. Darly, alongside her husband Matthew, took up the art of caricature - cartoonish drawings relying on exaggerated features intended to mock or satirise the subject - from Italy. She drew, printed and sold her caricatures from her shop on Fleet Street, taking advantage of the vogue for satire, scandal and gossip that were selling newspapers, and soon became the most prominent of a number of female printmakers and sellers.

In the 1760s, it was almost always politics that was the domain of satirical prints, but by the 1770s, targets had expanded to include high society and fashion. The caricatures and cartoons were most often sold as individual prints, from specialist printers like the Darlys, and would be bought by relatively wealthy people and shared among their peers. Often, even if people couldn't afford to purchase the prints themselves, they'd be able to enjoy them in coffee houses and inns, which would purchase prints and newspapers for their customers to read, share and discuss. Topical prints would even be placed in the windows poking fun at public figures like the Prince Regent, spreading their reach even further.

The popularity of these satirical prints was unprecedented, and a number of artists achieved great renown and acclaim, the foremost of whom was James Gillray. Gillray is still considered one of the greatest political cartoonists of all time, and

> "Writers would focus on a particular society couple – no names were mentioned but there were heavy hints as to their identities – to be profiled and have their love lives and scandals exposed"

James Gillray's most famous print, 'The Plumb-Pudding in Danger', showing William Pitt and Napoleon carving up the globe between them

SCANDAL, SATIRE AND THE PRESS

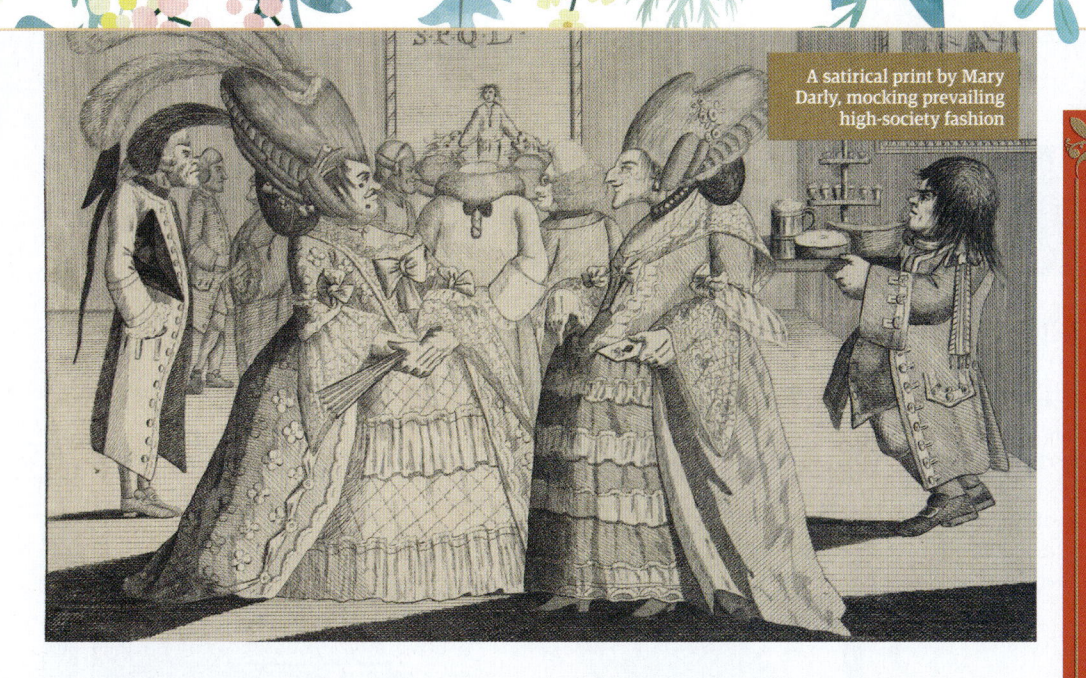

A satirical print by Mary Darly, mocking prevailing high-society fashion

his brightly hand-coloured etchings were near-ubiquitous in the late 18th century. Such was the power of his satire, the idea that Napoleon was short – an image that is still commonplace today – came from his depictions of the Frenchman. Napoleon himself recognised Gillray's influence, saying, while in exile, that the cartoonist did him more damage than a dozen generals.

Gillray and his contemporaries, such as Isaac Cruikshank, Thomas Rowlandson and Hannah Humphrey (as well as being a satirist herself, Humphrey was a printer and seller, who superseded Darly and published many of Gillray's prints), would often portray high society as frivolous and downright silly. Their mocking eye not only amused but directly affected how fashions came and went.

There was one last gossipy innovation that the Regency period had to offer in addition to scandal sheets, gossip columns and satirical prints: silver fork novels. These stories, also known as fashionable novels, were cheap books that were invariably set among the members of the aristocracy and depicted seedy stories of vice and scandal. They quickly gained popularity after the first, Theodore Hook's *Sayings and Doings*, was published in 1824.

Although they were always presented as fiction, many would be closely drawn from life, and successful authors, such as Lady Blessington, Catherine Gore and Lady Bury, were able to make a good living from them. Silver fork novels appealed not only to the upper and middle classes themselves, who were, as we've seen, particularly fond of gossip, but to other classes too, as they provided an insight into a fascinating, unimaginable and unattainable lifestyle.

The proliferation of media for the dissemination of gossip and scandal in the Georgian and Regency periods shows how important they were as entertainment and for creating and upholding social groups throughout England. These scandal sheets, newspaper columns and satires paved the way for the eventual emergence of the tabloids of the 20th century. The medium may change, but the insatiable appetite for gossip never fails.

Elizabeth Bride ('Miss B___e') and John Calcraft the Elder ('The Amorous Agent'), one of the couples discussed in Town and Country's *'Tête-à-Tête' column*

The Caricatures of George IV

No-one provided more material for Britain's satirists than the Prince Regent himself

As the most famous man in Britain, Prince George, the Prince Regent and later King George IV, was an easy and common target for satirists. George didn't help himself, as he was frequently inattentive to political concerns, prone to spending sprees and had a complicated personal life. In 1785, aged 21, a young George fell head-over-heels for a Catholic widow, Maria Fitzherbert. Banned from marrying a Catholic and from marrying without the King's permission, George married her in secret. As soon as the news broke, over 34 satirical prints were published about the scandal.

The Prince's subsequent marriage to his cousin, Caroline, which was sanctioned but reluctant to say the least, was further fodder for satirists, as was his eventual attempt in 1820, after the death of his father, to annul the marriage by accusing Caroline of adultery (despite his own repeated infidelity). George's parade of mistresses, careless spending and love of excess kept food on the tables of James Gillray, George Cruikshank and Thomas Rowlandson for years.

George behaviour made him a target for satirists throughout his adult life

SEX, LIES AND DUELS

Welcome to the scandals that besmirched the great and good of Regency Britain

WRITTEN BY **SCOTT REEVES**

The Prince Regent was a man known to attract attention of a scandalous sort, but he wasn't the only topic of gossip. His subjects liked a secret love affair or public spat too, and even the Prime Minister and hero of Waterloo himself hit the headlines for all the wrong reasons. Join us as we dish the dirt on the Regency scandals that were the tabloid fodder of their day.

THE CASTLEREAGH –CANNING DUEL
The politicians who turned on each other
21 SEPTEMBER 1809

The debates around the table at 10 Downing Street got heated during the government of the Duke of Portland. Minister of War Viscount Castlereagh and Foreign Secretary George Canning blamed each other for Britain's struggles in the war against Napoleon, and the ill-feeling got so bad that Castlereagh demanded Canning face him in a duel on Portland Heath. The odds were against Canning, who'd never fired a gun before, and he went down with a bullet in his thigh. Though Canning survived, the fact that two leading politicians had fought a duel caused an outcry that only ended with the resignation of the Prime Minister, as he had failed to control his ministers.

In 1827, long after the dust settled, Canning became prime minister - but he died 119 days after taking office

Visitors to Eleanor and Sarah's home included fellow scandalites the Duke of Wellington and Lord Byron

THE LADIES OF LLANGOLLEN
The lesbian power couple
1780-1829

Irish aristocratic daughters Eleanor Butler and Sarah Ponsonby had no intention of following the life expected of them. Rather than marry into the correct social circles, they decided to flee Ireland together and dressed as men. Although their escape attempt was thwarted, Butler and Ponsonby's love for each other remained strong. Eventually, their families relented and allowed them to set up home together in Wales. Butler and Ponsonby became minor celebrities and hosted many wealthy visitors over their 49-year relationship, many of whom were curious about the two women's eccentric lifestyle. At a time when male homosexuality was illegal, female homosexuality was regarded as a peculiarity and the law treated it more leniently.

SEX, LIES AND DUELS

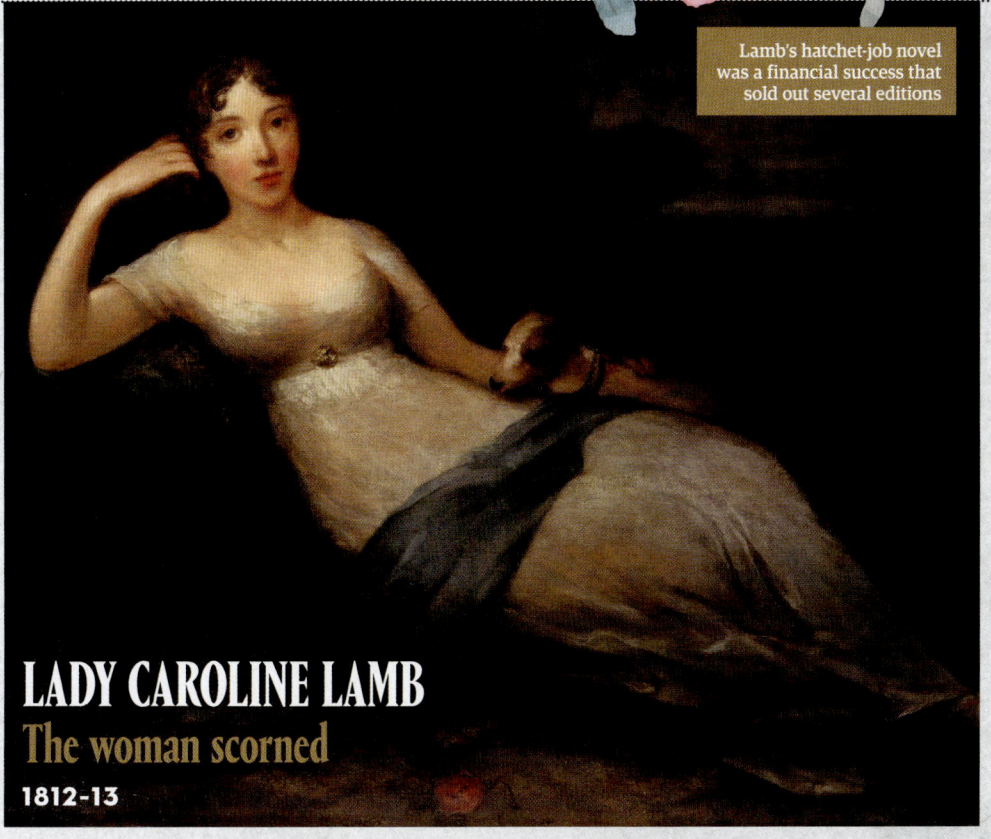

Lamb's hatchet-job novel was a financial success that sold out several editions

LADY CAROLINE LAMB
The woman scorned
1812-13

Although she was married to a rising politician, Lady Caroline Lamb began a public affair with Lord Byron in the summer of 1812 - but when Byron called it off, Lady Lamb took the news very badly indeed. She slashed her wrists with a broken glass at a society ball and stalked him through London's streets. Later, she penned a novel featuring a thinly disguised version of Byron who betrays those around him. Lady Lamb was also the one to coin the infamous phrase that Byron was "mad, bad and dangerous to know".

Winchelsea's criticism didn't have an effect, and the Catholic Emancipation Act became law a few weeks later

THE WELLINGTON-WINCHELSEA DUEL
The pistol-wielding prime minister
21 MARCH 1829

The Earl of Winchelsea didn't approve of plans to restore civil rights to Catholics during the Duke of Wellington's first term as prime minister, and his criticism got so bad that Wellington challenged him to a duel. They met at Battersea, where Winchelsea refused to fire. Wellington took his shot but missed. He always claimed that he fired wide on purpose, but many suspect the hero of Waterloo was actually just a bad marksman.

BYRON'S INCESTUOUS AFFAIR
The bed hopping lord
1814-16

When Augusta Leigh gave birth to her third child in 1814, it should have been a cause for celebration. Instead, it set tongues wagging. Many thought that the baby's father wasn't her husband, but her half-brother: poet and playboy Lord Byron. The rumours threatened to besmirch Byron's already notorious reputation, and he tried to quash the gossip by marrying Annabella Milbanke in January 1815. It didn't work. The newlyweds separated a year later, with Milbanke accusing Byron of incest, homosexuality and sodomy - all three of which were illegal. The short marriage did at least result in the birth of a daughter who'd grow up to be famed computing pioneer, Ada Lovelace.

After the end of his marriage, Byron fled abroad to avoid prosecution and never returned to England

SOCIETY & SCANDAL

Gin Lane by William Hogarth, 1751. An engraving created to demonstrate the evils of gin and what it did to society - squalor, death and desperation

THE REGENCY UNDERWORLD

As populations boomed in a time with almost no official policing, a powder keg of crime exposed Regency Britain's dark side

WRITTEN BY **EMMA SLATTERY WILLIAMS**

While the Regency period is often celebrated for its glamorous balls and elegance, a shadowy world of crime lurked just beneath the surface – a stark contrast to the genteel façade that is often conjured by the many cultural depictions that portray the era. It didn't take much to scratch beneath the quaint charm of afternoon teas to unearth a pervasive dark underbelly.

As in any era across history, there were the rich and prosperous (such as many of the characters in the Netflix show, *Bridgerton*) and there were the working classes who had to do all they could to avoid poverty. Then below them were those who existed in the criminal world – some out of choice and others from necessity. Gambling, thieving and prostitution all flourished in the hidden corners of society, unnoticed by those busy sipping tea in their comfortable homes.

The Prince Regent, later King George IV, exemplified the era's contradictions with his well-documented vices: womanising, heavy drinking, and gambling – all stark contrasts to the respectability associated with the period. You only have to look at some of the legislation that was brought in during, or immediately after, the Regency era to get a feel of what went on – the Metropolitan Police Act of 1829, which created the first professional full-time police force in London, and the Anatomy Act of 1832, which aimed to halt the disturbing and illegal trade in corpses.

London exemplified the two worlds existing together. With its amalgamation of old and new, you could be walking down a respectable road in the capital one moment and then find yourself in squalid slums surrounded by gin palaces, brothels and pawnbrokers the next, with the stench of sewage filling the air. The population was growing at a rapid rate thanks to the industrial advances pushing people into the cities. Housing couldn't be built fast enough, so families would be packed together in unhygienic squalor. Between 1801 and 1820, the population of London rose by a quarter of a million. This was happening in other cities as well – in Liverpool, though not as unwieldy as the capital, the population grew 16 times by 1801, compared to the previous century.

Some of the poorer districts of London were known as 'rookeries' as they resembled how a rook would nest and were chaotic with people living on top of each other. St Giles was a notorious rookery and became a breeding ground for criminality, which lawmen and gentleman alike took pains to avoid, with its maze of dingy alleyways.

SOCIETY & SCANDAL

Many of these areas were home to flash-houses – pubs frequented by criminals that also provided shelter for runaway children. But the shelter wasn't provided out of an act of kindness. The children were often educated in the arts of theft and prostitution. By 1807, estimates suggested that one in five women in London were involved in prostitution in some form.

Lax laws around alcohol meant that extremely cheap gin was easy to buy and by the middle of the 18th century, there was around one public house to every 15 houses in London alone. As well as being the epicentre for criminal gangs and violence, they could also lead those who grew dependent on alcohol to be forced into crime or prostitution as a way to feed their habit.

Desperate circumstances often forced children into a life of crime in order to support their family, or simply because they had no family. Sadly, a life of crime was potentially a better deal than the alternative industries children were employed in, for example the climbing boys – apprentices to a chimney sweep who were sent up chimneys to remove blockages. If they weren't burned in the process, they could be abused or threatened into going up claustrophobic soot-filled chimneys. Runaway children were prime targets for criminal gangs who would recruit them as footpads (thieves), pickpockets or useful distractions. Their young age or troubled circumstances wouldn't necessarily save them from the hangman's noose, either. The idea that a child didn't fully comprehend criminal responsibility was not established at this time, so children from the age of seven could be sentenced to death – though in many cases these did end up being commuted.

It wasn't just cities that had an element of danger: the open road could also pose a risk. The highwayman, seen by some as a romantic Robin Hood figure preying on the underserving wealthy, was on the decline during the Regency period but the danger was still there. During the 18th century these thieves were a menace to the traveller – holding up carriages at the end of a pistol. Places like Hounslow Heath, where roads led from London to Bath and Exeter, were notoriously dangerous. The time of highwaymen began to come to an end as populations grew and more land was built on, making it harder for them to get away unseen. Currency also began to be traceable, as banknotes were preferred over gold, making thieving a much harder endeavour.

Crime flourished, which meant that so did the need for order. Each parish was supposed to have a constable, but this was a voluntary position done in the post-holder's spare time and it could be costly for those looking to have a crime investigated. People could hire thief-takers, akin to today's bounty hunters, to hunt down a suspect but you risked them extorting the criminal in exchange for not handing them over, or even setting up crimes themselves to gain work.

There was no cohesive court system, so bringing someone to justice could be a lengthy process.

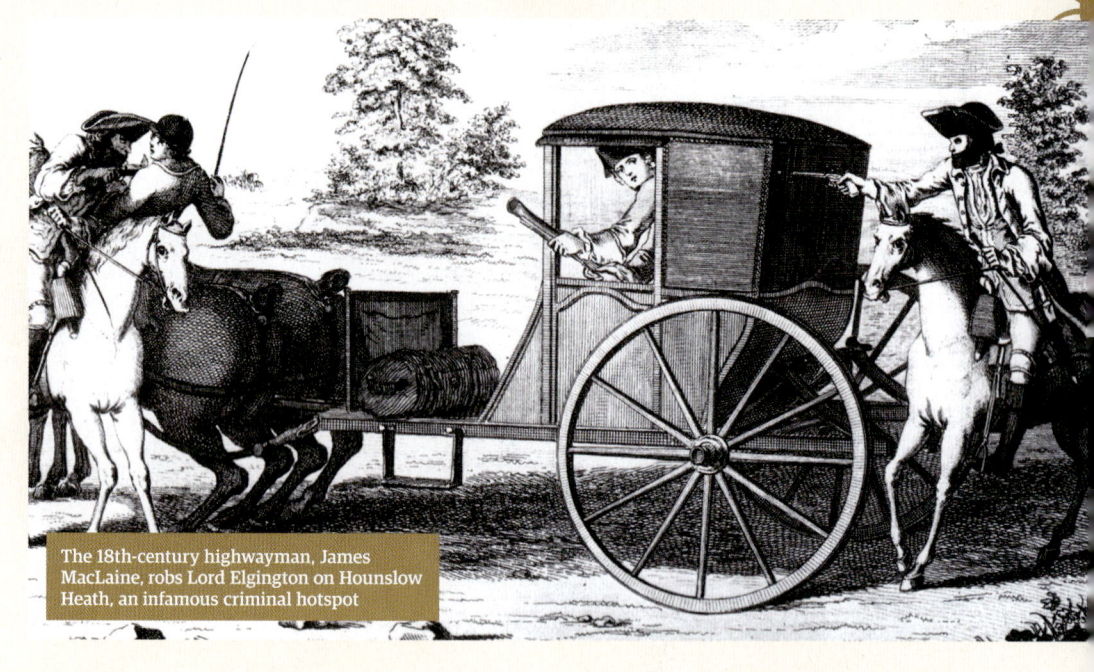

The 18th-century highwayman, James MacLaine, robs Lord Elgington on Hounslow Heath, an infamous criminal hotspot

> *"Desperate circumstances forced children into a life of crime in to support their family, or simply because they had no family"*

Snatching Bodies In Scotland
Uncover the gruesome and illicit profession of grave robbing

Lurking in the dark corners of graveyards, a sinister trade unfolded – a desperate scramble for bodies, where the dead had become commodities. The practice of body snatching (digging up corpses) saw a disturbing rise during the Georgian period due to a shortage of cadavers for medical study. Despite the 1751 Murder Act, which saw the bodies of convicted murderers sent to medical schools, medical advances were such that the justice systems couldn't provide the numbers needed.

Surgeons sought fresh bodies and were willing to pay, leading to the rise of 'resurrectionists,' who would illegally exhume corpses, often working quickly and stealthily under the cover of night. Families, desperate to ensure their loved ones' resting places remained undisturbed, would surround graves with iron cages and some churchyards even built watchtowers to dissuade would-be body snatchers. It wasn't long, however, until some turned to murder in order to provide a fresh supply – the most notorious of these were Edinburgh's William Burke and William Hare.

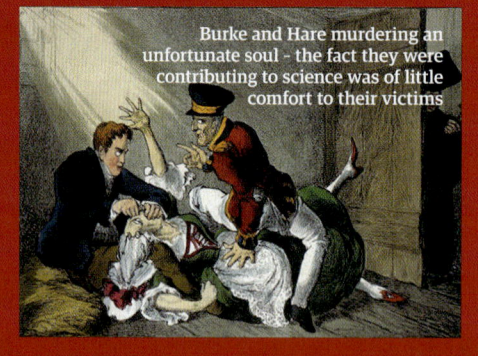

Burke and Hare murdering an unfortunate soul - the fact they were contributing to science was of little comfort to their victims

Between 1827 and 1828 it is believed they killed 16 people and sold their bodies. They were eventually caught, and Hare testified against Burke leading to his execution. In a bitter twist of irony, Burke's body was used in anatomy lessons and his skeleton can still be seen at Edinburgh's Surgeons' Hall. Hare was eventually released, and his final fate remains unknown.

In 1832, the Anatomy Act was passed, which allowed lawful access to unclaimed bodies from workhouses and hospitals, effectively ending the body-snatching era while acknowledging its role in advancing medical science.

THE REGENCY UNDERWORLD

Crowds gathered at the pillory at Charing Cross, 1809, to watch justice being served

A portrait from 1805 showing London's floating prison ships - used due to overcrowding

Judges heard the most serious crimes at the Courts of Assizes in six courts across the country, while lesser crimes were heard by magistrates in Petty Sessions - local courts that were held a few times throughout the year.

In 1749, novelist and magistrate Henry Fielding, along with his half-brother John Fielding, established the Bow Street Runners - a paid police force based out of his Bow Street Magistrate Court. Armed with a stick, pistol and handcuffs they were paid a guinea a week to catch criminals and would gain a bonus for successful convictions. What started out as six members became 68 by the turn of the 19th century. Their success soon saw this idea adapted across other areas of London. John Fielding also established a newspaper called *The Quarterly Pursuit*, renamed *The Public Hue and Cry* in 1786. This contained announcements of stolen property and criminal suspects along with their nefarious deeds - it wasn't taken up nationally, but it fuelled the public's intrigue for reading salacious tales of criminals.

By the end of the Regency era a centralised police force was established in London thanks to the 1829 Metropolitan Police Act, which initially recruited 3,200 men to be trained as full-time policemen. By the next decade, towns outside the capital were given powers to set up their own police force.

By the end of the 18th century, the law punished around 200 crimes with death - this included murder, robbery, cattle stealing and even what today would be seen as minor crimes against property, such as the cutting down of trees and the destruction of fish ponds. Advocates faced resistance when they called for the removal of these harsher sentences, though in reality magistrates would often quietly commute these sentences to transportation or imprisonment. In 1808, lawmakers downgraded pickpocketing, which was rife in Britain's cities, from a capital offence. Prosecutions then rose, which prompted those in favour of capital punishment to suggest more lenient punishments led to an increase in crime, rather than a rise in poverty.

From 1783, public executions began being held outside Newgate Prison and these drew huge crowds, which continued well into the Victorian era - whether to jeer the villain or weep for the death of a popular outlaw. The spectacle of criminals at the stocks and whipping posts were well attended too, illustrating how much the public enjoyed watching justice be served.

POLITICS & POWER

056 **THE TORIES IN POWER**

060 **MURDER OF THE PRIME MINISTER**

062 **REMEMBERING PETERLOO**

070 **BRITAIN AT WAR**

074 **BATTLE OF WATERLOO**

078 **THE WAR ON SLAVERY**

POLITICS & POWER

THE TORIES IN POWER

During the turbulent years of the Regency era, the Tories and the Whigs did battle across the Commons chamber

WRITTEN BY **CATHERINE CURZON**

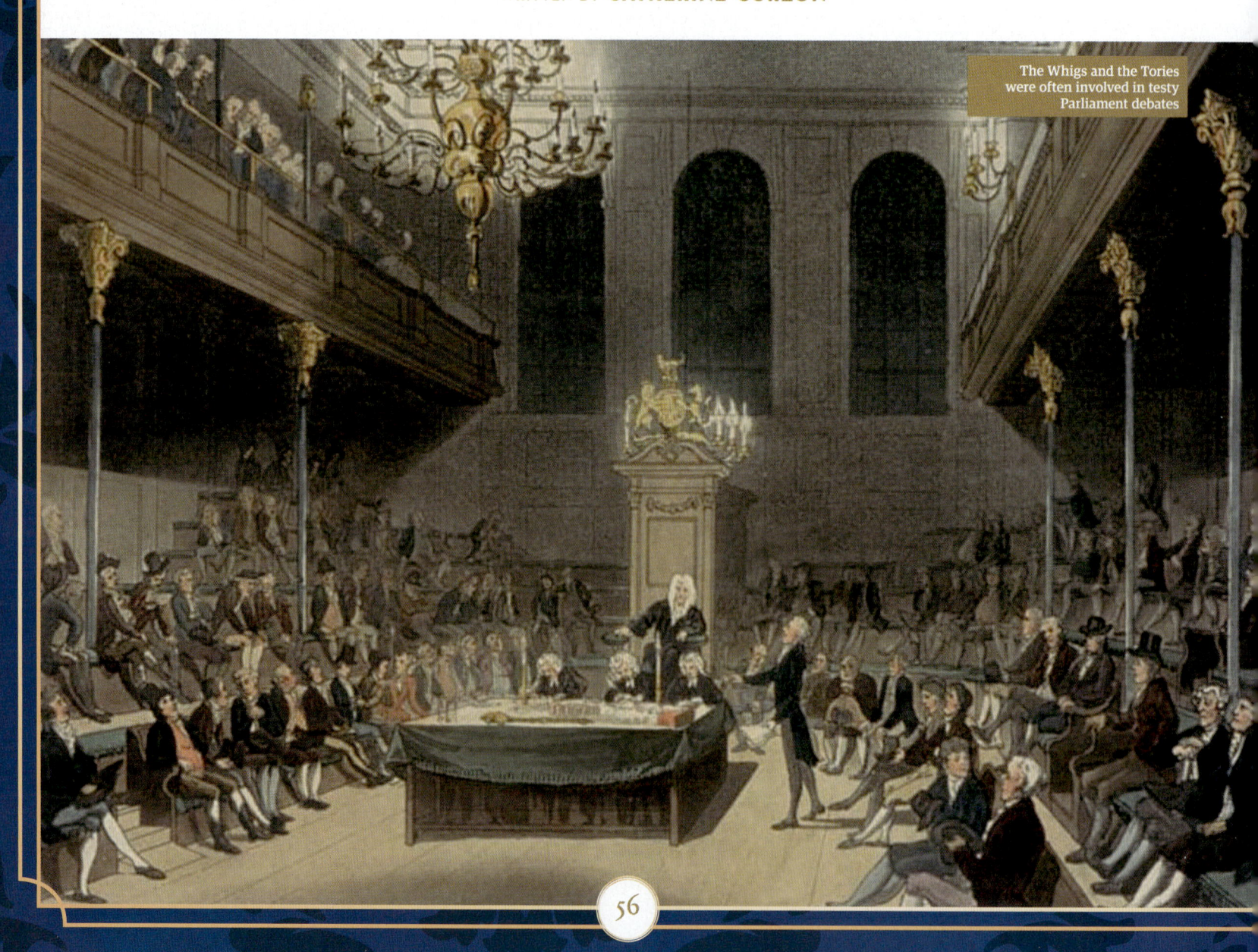

The Whigs and the Tories were often involved in testy Parliament debates

THE TORIES IN POWER

Throughout the Georgian era, there were two dominant parties in British politics: the Whigs and the Tories. While the Whigs had been the party of government for the majority of the reigns of the first two Georges, it was the Tories who sat in power for most of George III's reign. The party came to government in 1762 under the leadership of Lord Bute, who had served as young George III's mentor when his father had died, leading to allegations of favouritism and cronyism. George, however, was a Tory to his very bones, and remained loyal to the party for his entire life. However, his son and heir, the Prince of Wales, later Prince Regent and King George IV, was anything but. He was an avowed Whig, who many feared would kick out the Tories and install his own preferred party the minute that he assumed power. In the event, he did not, and the Tories ran every administration from December 1783 to November 1830, with the exception of 1806's Ministry of All the Talents, which saw Whigs and Tories join forces during the dark days of war.

The fierce battle between the Whigs and the Tories during George III's reign was best illustrated by the similarly infamous clashes between Tory prime minister, William Pitt the Younger, and Whig leader, Charles James Fox, the Prince's close friend. The Tories were monarchists who believed that the sovereign should play a vital role in the inner workings of government. The Whigs, however, believed Parliament should have more power than any monarch, thus representing not the wishes of the elite and the powerful church, but the man and woman in the street. Crucially, they promised voting and parliamentary reform.

Both Pitt and Fox died in 1806 and by the time of the Regency era, Spencer Perceval was prime minister. Upon his assassination in 1812, the position was taken by Lord Liverpool, who presided over a hardline administration and a country in crisis. He packed his cabinet with Tory bigwigs, including the troubled Viscount Castlereagh as foreign secretary and Earl Bathurst at the War Office. Privileged, old school and devoted to their party, there would be little room for dissent.

The early years of Liverpool's tenure were dominated by the War of 1812 and the closing years of the Napoleonic Wars. While the 1815 victory at Waterloo was a time of great rejoicing, it couldn't paper over the cracks in a country that was anything but a green and pleasant land. The Regent's carriage was pelted with stones as it passed through London, and someone daubed "Bread, or the Regent's head" on the wall of his opulent Carlton House home. Unemployment was rife and poverty widespread, yet taxes on every item you could imagine seemed to be rising. With only 11 per cent of all men eligible to vote and most of them in the south, England was a powder keg primed to explode.

One of the reasons for unemployment was mechanisation of labour thanks to the Industrial Revolution, with workers laid off and replaced by machines. In northern counties, a protest movement sprang up in the form of the Luddites, who smashed the machines and committed other acts of sabotage and organised protest. In reply, the government sent out troops to crush the dissenters, resulting in arrests and a mass trial. Though many were acquitted, punishments ranging from execution to transportation eventually put a stop to the Luddites.

Lord Liverpool presided over a hardline government that rejected the very notion of parliamentary reform

"The Tory government was regarded as for the elite... as far as the people could see, the Tories were happy to watch them starve"

In 1815, rioters besieged the door of the House of Commons in response to the Corn Laws

The Tory government was regarded not as a government for the people, but the elite, and few things did more to cement this than the 1815 Corn Laws. Fearing that cheap foreign grain would overwhelm the British market, the government passed a law that imposed sky-high tariffs on grain import, even when domestic crops were poor. The Corn Laws benefitted landowners greatly, raising food prices at a time when many were already struggling. The result was riots, especially after 1816, the so-called Year Without a Summer, led to a disastrous harvest. As famine raged among the poorest, still the price of bread remained artificially high. As far as the people could see, the Tories were happy to watch them starve.

Lord Liverpool, meanwhile, further cemented his hardline reputation in August 1819, when protestors gathered at St Peter's Field in Manchester to demand parliamentary reform. Though the gathering was peaceful, magistrates ordered a cavalry charge on the men, women and children who had come out to protest. Led by a

POLITICS & POWER

The Reform Act was finally passed in 1832

prominent northern Tory, the charge cut down the attendees without mercy. Eighteen people died in what became known as the Peterloo Massacre, and hundreds more were injured.

After the Peterloo Massacre, protests swept the north, calling for justice. However the government's response was not one of sympathy and there was certainly no hope of reform. Instead, Lord Liverpool acted swiftly to prevent any future such protests by introducing the Six Acts. These were a knee-jerk reaction aimed at suppressing any action that aimed to promote radical reform. On 23 November, the home secretary, Henry Addington, introduced the acts, and by the end of 1819, they were law. The Six Acts made it illegal for any meeting to teach military training; awarded magistrates powers to seize privately-owned weapons and arrest the owners; sped up court processing; banned meetings of more than 50 people; gagged radical authors and the radical press; and imposed heavy taxes on publications that disseminated radical opinion.

These acts were seen as final proof of the oppressive nature of the Tory government and its refusal to give the working classes any quarter whatsoever. For the next decade the calls for reform grew and were met with stony disregard, and when the Duke of Wellington became Tory prime minister in 1828, he made it known that he was utterly opposed to any such move. However, with riots and protests gripping the country and the Whigs promising reform, Wellington's party knew that the writing was on the wall. He lost a vote of no confidence in November 1830 and was forced to resign. He was replaced by Whig Lord Grey, a dedicated reformer, who promised in his first speech as the prime minister that things would change.

Under the existing system, a man had to own property or pay specific taxes to have a vote, thus excluding most outside of the upper classes. Prime Minister Grey swore to change that and though the first two reform bills failed to make it through the Tory blockade in Parliament, in 1832 the Reform Act succeeded. In fact, it was political chicanery that got the vote through, as Lord Grey planned to ask King William IV to create new Whig peers in the House of Lords, thus guaranteeing that the bill would be passed. Upon hearing of this scheme, Tory peers abstained, thereby ensuring that it would pass but that no fresh Whig peers would be required.

The Luddites took their name from the folkloric character, Ned Ludd, who became their figurehead

THE LEADER of the LUDDITES

THE TORIES IN POWER

The Cato Street Conspiracy
In 1820, an audacious plot aimed to wipe out the Prime Minister and his cabinet

On 23 February 1820, nearly 30 conspirators who called themselves the Spencean Philanthropists gathered in a cowshed on London's Cato Street, primed to commit murder. The leader of the conspiracy was radical activist, Arthur Thistlewood. Unknown to him, though, his most trusted lieutenant, George Edwards, was an informant reporting directly to the Home Secretary.

Furious at the government's disregard of the working classes, the conspirators planned to storm a dinner at the home of Lord Harrowby, where the entire cabinet and prime minister, Lord Liverpool, would be present. There they would murder the attendees, then display the heads of their victims on Westminster Bridge. This, they believed would cause the people to revolt against the oppressive government regime. As the armed conspirators huddled on Cato Street waiting for the dinner to commence, a team of Bow Street Runners burst into the shed to arrest them. In all the commotion, Thistlewood fatally stabbed one of the Runners, Richard Smithers, who ended up being the only fatality of the Cato Street Conspiracy.

During the trial, two members of the conspiracy testified against their peers in exchange for clemency. Charged with high treason, most of the men were sentenced to be hanged, drawn and quartered, but the majority of these were later commuted to hanging and beheading, with three commuted to transportation for life.

The Cato Street Conspiracy was thwarted by the Bow Street Runners

Tired of social divisions, protestors scrawled "Bread, or the Regent's head" on the wall of the Prince Regent's palatial home

The Reform Act, however, did not bring the great change people had hoped for. It redrew borough and constituency boundaries to combat fraud and rotten boroughs, expanded the caveat regarding property ownership to include tenant farmers, small landowners and shopkeepers, and gave the vote to all householders who paid a yearly rental of £10 or more. Sadly the act also excluded all women from voting.

Though the act left many men disappointed that they still were not eligible to vote, it at least proved that change was possible, when the Tories had for so long sworn that it was not. It was a starting point and over the decades, the calls for reform grew louder and louder, until they could no longer be ignored.

Once the seemingly immovable party of government, the Tory party entered its twilight with the fall of the Wellington administration. It would eventually fade completely under the leadership of Robert Peel who, in December 1834, issued his Tamworth Manifesto, in which he outlined the principles of the modern Conservative Party. From the ashes of the Tories the new party grew, even though it still carries its old Tory monicker to this day.

POLITICS & POWER

Domestic Disorder

With tensions rising, it was feared that rebellion wasn't far away

Spencer Perceval was prime minister from 1809 to 1812 and at the time of his assassination, Britain had been going through a period of political unrest. The Luddite movement, a group of textile workers who feared that the introduction of machinery put their livelihoods at risk, had emerged in northern England, breaking into factories and destroying machines. It did not help that Britain was also at war with France, which intensified economic pressure and led to increased poverty in some areas of the country.

This situation worsened thanks to the Orders in Council, a series of restrictions placed on French trade in response to the war, which were extremely unpopular with Englishmen who claimed that they were ruining their trade. On the day of Perceval's assassination, he had arrived at the House of Commons to attend an inquiry into the effect the Orders were having domestically and whether they should be repealed.

Considering the tension in Britain at the time, it is unsurprising that immediately after Perceval's assassination, there was a concern in Parliament that his death was the start of a widespread rebellion and that Bellingham may have had accomplices lurking around - especially as a mob attempted to free him as he was escorted to Newgate Prison.

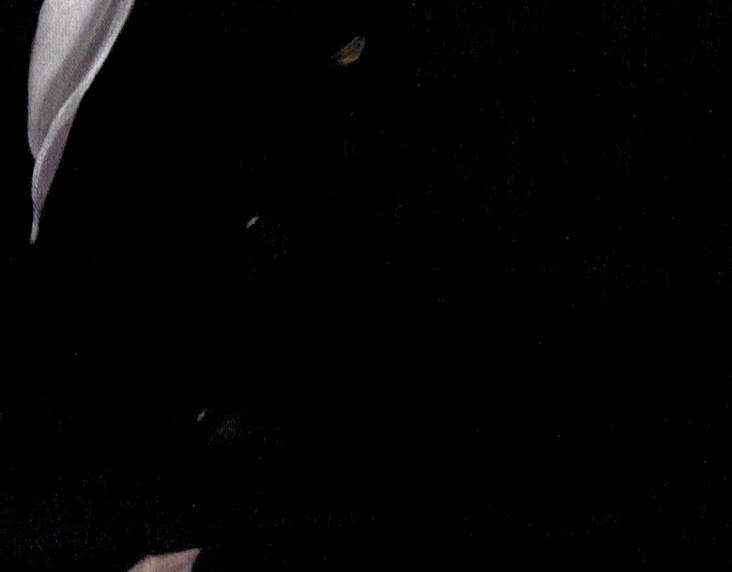

An engraving of a Luddite leader from 1812

Perceval was the British prime minister from 1809 to 1812

MURDER OF THE PRIME MINISTER

How Spencer Perceval lost his life at the hands of a calculated murderer hell-bent on revenge

WRITTEN BY **JESSICA LEGGETT**

It was 5.15pm, on 11 May 1812, and the British prime minister, Spencer Perceval, was running late. Stepping into the lobby of the House of Commons and removing his coat, Perceval took a few steps forward before a man wearing an overcoat approached him, having risen from his seat next to the fireplace nearby. Taking out a pistol, the man pointed it at Perceval and shot a bullet right into his chest. Staggering forward, Perceval gasped, "I am murdered," before collapsing face down in front of a shocked MP, with men rushing to help him. Meanwhile, the assassin calmly returned to his seat by the fireplace and waited for his arrest.

The assassin, John Bellingham, was a failed businessman in his 40s from Liverpool, who had held a grudge against the government for years. He had been arrested at the Russian port of Arkhangelsk for debt in 1804, spending the next five years in prison. Bellingham insisted that he had been set up by two disgruntled Russian merchants, but his pleas of innocence were ignored. Returning to England in 1809 and struggling financially, Bellingham was furious about the lack of assistance that he had received from the British government, in particular from Granville Leveson-Gower, the ambassador in Saint Petersburg.

For the next three years, he repeatedly petitioned Perceval, the Prince Regent, the treasury and the Privy Council demanding that they address his case and award him compensation, but he was rebuffed. Infuriated and desperate, Bellingham decided that assassinating Perceval was the only way he would be heard. In preparation, he bought two pistols in Skinner Street and got a tailor to make a special nine-inch pocket inside his overcoat to accommodate one of them, before spending the next few weeks visiting the House of Commons and observing the members of Parliament.

After Perceval was shot, he was carried into the Speaker's apartments nearby but succumbed to his injuries just minutes later. Surrendering himself willingly, Bellingham was searched and his second pistol was found before he was escorted to the bar of the House and arrested. News of the assassination spread quickly and sent shockwaves through Parliament, with surviving notes from the day recording that the Lord Chancellor had told the House of Lords: "A most melancholy and atrocious circumstance had taken place in the Lobby of the Lower House of Parliament." While the House of Commons was adjourned until the next day, the House of Lords ordered that no one could leave the premises while a witness to the murder, a solicitor, was questioned.

At midnight, Bellingham was taken to Newgate Prison and three days later, he was put on trial for murder at the Old Bailey. Admitting that he would rather have killed Leveson-Gower, Bellingham also gave a statement in which he hoped that the assassination would serve as "a warning to all future ministers and that they will henceforth do the thing that is right". Despite his lawyer's plea of insanity, Bellingham was found guilty and he was hanged on 18 May at the prison.

In the wake of Perceval's death, both the Lords and Commons agreed to arrange financial provision for his family. Parliament passed an act that same year granting the family £50,000 and awarding Perceval's widow, Jane, an annual sum of £2,000. Although Perceval's death was mourned by many, some expressed joy at his assassination, particularly in areas of the country that were suffering from economic hardship due to the Napoleonic Wars.

Perceval was succeeded by another fellow Tory, Robert Jenkinson, 2nd Earl of Liverpool, and the policies from his administration were quickly reversed. Aside from a handful of monuments erected in his honour, including one in Westminster Abbey commissioned by Parliament in 1814, Perceval's death ultimately caused little impact and he has since largely been forgotten, save for the circumstances in which he lost his life.

"Infuriated and desperate, Bellingham decided that assassinating Perceval was the only way that he would be heard"

POLITICS & POWER

*This feature was written in 2019 to mark the 200-year anniversary of the Peterloo Massacre. Any events/exhibitions mentioned will no longer be running. However, the peterloo1819.co.uk website remains active

REMEMBERING PETERLOO

We speak with historians, curators and campaigners about why it's so important we never forget the 200-year* old tragedy of this protest for voting rights

WRITTEN BY **JONATHAN GORDON & TOM GARNER**

16 August 1819: between 60,000-80,000 men, women and children assembled in St Peter's Field in Manchester to protest for their right to parliamentary representation. Not long after Henry Hunt, the famed orator, took to the hustings the local magistrates ordered the arrest of Hunt and those leading the protest, and the Manchester and Salford Yeomanry charged the field, attacking with sabres as they met resistance from the crowd. With tensions rising they were followed by the 15th Hussars, who also charged having been ordered to disperse the assembly. What they seemingly didn't know was that exits had been blocked and most in the field were now trapped. It's believed that 18 people died in the attack, including one two-year-old child, with over 500 injured. It was a shocking event that the press nicknamed "Peterloo" as an ironic reference to the Battle of Waterloo. John Lees, a former soldier and textiles worker, died from wounds he sustained and is reported to have told a friend before his death, "At Waterloo there was man to man but there it was downright murder."

It's an event that echoed through the years that followed, but it would not be until 1832 and the Great Reform Act that anything close to what protestors called for would be put into law and over 100 years before universal suffrage would finally be achieved in Britain.

We spoke with some of the people looking to keep the memory of the Peterloo Massacre alive and why they think it is such an important moment in British history.

"Between 1819 and 1832, there were several hundred petitions sent into parliament from people who were there demanding an inquiry"

REMEMBERING PETERLOO

Peterloo and Manchester Histories

Mike Leigh's film, *Peterloo*, brought the events of 1819 to life with to the day of protest as well as the gruesome events that followed

KAREN SHANNON
Chief Executive

How long have you been working on the various events you have planned for the anniversary?
Manchester Histories and partners, which include both large cultural organisations and small community groups across Greater Manchester, have been working over the past four years on the programme that has led to Peterloo 2019. This has included running regular network and planning meetings to shape what activities take place and to develop the different strands of work such as the learning resources and the new website (peterloo1819.co.uk), which will also form part of the legacy for the project.

Did you have a particular mission statement for what you wanted to achieve for the anniversary?
Despite the scale of the Peterloo Massacre and the impact that it had at the time, both nationally and internationally, awareness levels have remained low. Peterloo is a chapter of our history that links directly to our present and events that followed like the Chartist and suffragette movements, with ordinary people campaigning for change. Our mission has been to make people more aware of the story and the relevance of Peterloo, to bring this to life and to explore the impact on society both then and now.

You've approached this anniversary in a multitude of ways, one of which is a broader series of events around protest and freedom of speech in the 200 years since Peterloo. Why did you choose to do that?
We want to make sure Peterloo has relevance to today and to influence people's future thinking in terms of finding out about their own and others' histories and heritage. The themes were chosen so that people could talk about their own interests today in parallel to the events of Peterloo.

By also looking more broadly at protest, it's given us the opportunity to not just focus on the story of Peterloo but also other important events that have shaped our society today, like the Greenham Common Women's Peace Camp [established in 1981] that peacefully protested for nuclear disarmament.

What does Peterloo mean to the city of Manchester?
I think the commemorations to date have been very emotive. The Peterloo story unleashes a rawness, it stirs deep feelings of pride, anger, and highlights people's struggles to be represented. People have really connected to this and to each other through discussions and attending different events. It means Manchester is still a city that has lots to say and is proud of its radical roots and spirit!

St Peter's Field has since been built over, but Free Trade House is now roughly in that location

63

POLITICS & POWER

The Peterloo Veterans

The Peterloo Veterans, 27 September 1884: David Hilton, Thomas Chadderton, John Davies, Thomas Ogden, Jonathan Dawson, Susannah Whittaker, Mary Collins, Catherine McMurdo, Richard Waters, Thomas Schofield, Alice Schofield

MICHAEL WOOD
Historian

On 27 September 1884, an extraordinary photograph was taken of 11 elderly survivors of the Peterloo Massacre. Aged between 79 and 83, these protestors were still campaigning for better voting rights. A copy was discovered by historian and television presenter Michael Wood in a collection of old history books that belonged to his father. He recently gave a lecture about the image called 'The Peterloo Photograph' as part of Manchester Histories' bicentenary commemorations. We spoke to Wood about the massacre's powerful legacy in the city and beyond.

What did the march to St Peter's Field say about the condition of Manchester at the time?
There were massive divisions emerging with poverty and unemployment. The Industrial Revolution was underway and there were a lot of stresses and strains on society. Manchester was also a really difficult place to operate in. There was no civic order and it was still under a manorial ownership.

How important was the Peterloo Massacre as a political event?
One historian said that Peterloo was "up there with Magna Carta", so it was a massive moment and everybody recognised it. The leadership had instructed the protestors that there was to be absolutely no violence used or any semblance of rioting. There were a large number of women present, and Samuel Bamford described many of them as wearing white dresses and frocks with hats and garlands of flowers. The whole atmosphere was like Wakes Week with the festive summer entertainments that they put on in rural districts.

Everybody was therefore totally stunned by what happened. The government moved against reforming newspapers as often as it could but everybody was writing about it. Alison Morgan has just published a collection of Peterloo songs and ballads and she's retrieved about 80 to 90 of them! These were written in the immediate aftermath and sung in pubs, clubs and taverns. *The Manchester Guardian* (now *The Guardian*) was also founded in the aftermath of Peterloo.

Contemporary artwork depicting the tragic events

How was Peterloo remembered when you were growing up in Manchester?
Everybody knew about Peterloo in our neck of the woods. Certainly when I went up to Manchester Grammar School when I was 11 the history teacher made a speech on the first day. He gave us his pen-portrait of Manchester, which was a city of free trade, the Industrial Revolution and the heroes and heroines of Peterloo.

It was definitely something that we all knew about, and in my particular case my father came from Failsworth, which played quite a role in the Peterloo story. It was a famous centre of radicalism, and it was a really well-known story in our family because we've got ancestors tracing back there to at least the 1790s.

How did a copy of the 'Peterloo Photograph' come into your family?
These were 11 veterans who were youngsters at the time and they were all part of the Failsworth story. Our families were linked to a pool of people, including a few of the veterans, who went to Peterloo who were all neighbours, friends and related by marriage.

I should say that I'm no expert and these are simply family stories. As I was clearing out my mum's house after she died three years ago I found a box of books belonging to my dad that included photos and other odd and ends. We wondered why there were these old, obscure local history books of Failsworth among them and they all carried the photograph of the Peterloo veterans. My dad had kept three or four books that contained the picture because it was taken in Failsworth at a very prominent event.

What do we know about the photograph?
The account of the meeting from 1884 says that they carried a banner that they'd carried with Samuel Bamford's detachment to Peterloo. However, the two banners that you can read were from a demonstration for the vote that they had attended in 1884. There they are in their 80s and they are still fighting! They were still activists, and that night they went round to a local house for tea where they told stories and sang songs.

How important are photographs like this as historical records?
Photographs sometimes open an amazing window. There is quite a famous photograph in the British Library of a Chartist meeting in 1848 in Kennington, and when you have photos like that it's staggering. They are beyond price as a record of what people were actually like at that time during the early development of photography.

Photos can therefore be absolutely stunning and it's why I called my talk 'The Peterloo Photograph'. This is because you may think, "Peterloo? 1819? Photography wasn't invented then!" But there they are and we know who they were and what they did. They're no longer anonymous weavers who don't have any background or can't be placed.

How important are the bicentenary events for Manchester?
I think they are important and Manchester has always had a unique place in history. When you travel in on the train from Stockport it doesn't have the vibe of a great city of history or a place of destiny. However, because of what happened from the Industrial Revolution onwards, it was no mistake that so many movements began there. This included the suffragettes, and Chartism was really big in Manchester. It was a great centre of radical and liberal politics, and Friedrich Engels lived there, which is why Karl Marx came up.

It was really the experience of Manchester that led Engels and Marx to construe the nature of capitalism in the way that they did. If Engels had lived in Birmingham Marx would have seen a completely different kind of industrial society. It was made out of thousands of small workshops and it was a different kind of industrial economy altogether. Their interpretation of history was really influenced by Manchester.

Peterloo is ultimately a symbol, an electric moment after which nothing can be quite the same again. Mancunians still feel that and I think that's reflective of the pride they have in their city as a crucible of history where things are hammered out.

The growth of Manchester as the world's first city of the Industrial Revolution influenced many radical thinkers and movements including Karl Marx, the Chartists and the Suffragettes

The original Failsworth Pole, where people gathered, has since been replaced by a clock tower

POLITICS & POWER

Legacy of Peterloo

DR SHIRIN HIRSCH
Researcher at the People's History Museum and lecturer at Manchester Metropolitan University

The Disrupt? Peterloo and Protest exhibition at People's History Museum (PHM) is putting the Peterloo Massacre at the heart of a conversation about protest and collective action. Why was that important?
At People's History Museum (PHM) we wanted to remember the Peterloo Massacre as a critical event in modern Britain. But we also wanted to connect Peterloo with the present and future of protest and collective action rather than just a history lesson we wanted to think about how Peterloo influenced and inspired a much longer history of protest and resistance.

Did Peterloo set the stage for further protests for voting rights in the years that followed?
In the years following the massacre the government cracked down on protest. When Percy Bysshe Shelley heard of the massacre, he penned the poem *The Masque of Anarchy*, powerfully indicting those who were responsible. Yet Shelley could not find a publisher brave enough to print his words, with the genuine threat of imprisonment hanging over radicals in this period. It was only in 1832, after Shelley's death, that the poem was first published. Out of the ashes of Peterloo and following the Great Reform Act of 1832 a new working class movement emerged with the Chartists, and they would continue the struggle for voting rights that had been violently repressed at Peterloo.

Did the crackdown have a lasting effect on the memory of Peterloo?
Ordinary people continued to keep the memory of Peterloo alive. There were a huge number of protestors, around 60,000, who had witnessed the massacre and they refused to forget. In our collections and galleries at PHM, and now on show in our exhibition Disrupt? Peterloo and Protest, we hold many of these commemorative artefacts: handkerchiefs, jugs, flags and medals all made to continue the memory of Peterloo. But the repression that followed the massacre certainly means that many of these objects from the reform movement have now been lost or destroyed.

What do you feel Peterloo can teach us about modern protest?
The protestors who met at St Peter's Field powerfully represented the real communities of Manchester and its surrounding towns and villages. There were many women at the demonstration, and they often led their sections into the march. Women were critical to the reform movement, yet, just as now, they were mocked and targeted as they stepped out of their role as wives and mothers. Peterloo teaches us that the campaign for women's rights did not simply begin with the suffragettes. But the Peterloo Massacre also tells us that rights we have today, like the vote, were never simply given to us by enlightened governments. Instead, these rights were campaigned for by ordinary people, sometimes in dangerous circumstances amidst the brutality of the British Government.

"Peterloo teaches us that the campaign for women's rights did not simply begin with the suffragettes"

Thanks to Manchester being at the heart of the economic transformation of Britain it was also a hotbed of energised citizens looking to make their voices heard

Henry Hunt was a popular orator for the cause of parliamentary reform. He was arrested at Peterloo and imprisoned for two years

REMEMBERING PETERLOO

The view from Westminster

DAVID PRIOR
Head of Public Services and Outreach, Parliamentary Archives

The Six Acts, passed in 1819, were a direct response to the growing activism that had been showcased at Peterloo

What can visitors expect to find at the Parliament & Peterloo exhibition?
The Parliament & Peterloo exhibition, which opens on 4 July at Westminster Hall, really tells the story of how Parliament and Peterloo are connected. We look at the background of Peterloo and the state of the country immediately after the Battle of Waterloo. We also reference the beginnings of people campaigning for the right to vote.

One of the features we're having in the exhibition is an audiovisual presentation. We've been working in partnership with Royal Holloway University of London and they supplied us with some videos that bring to life some of the testimony of people who were around at the time. For instance, we have a video of someone who speaks the words of a woman called Mary Fildes who was actually one of the people on the platform with Henry Hunt at Peterloo.

What do we know about Westminster's understanding of what was happening in Manchester?
Because it was August, parliament wouldn't have been sitting at the time. Parliament as a body wasn't immediately aware of what was happening, but what happened subsequently was a series of reports and copies of letters from people who were there.

Between 1819 and at least 1832 there were several hundred petitions sent into parliament from people who were there demanding an inquiry.

Has the process of digitising your archive shed any new light on the response of parliament to Peterloo?
I think the papers we've found that are in the bundle marked 'papers relating to the internal state of the country' have possibly been overlooked by historians in the past, simply because of the way they've been catalogued here. There's a lot of personal testimony that I think sheds light on the way people were treated at the event.

Are there any examples of testimony that spring to mind?
Mary's is the testimony that I'm most aware of, and hers is that she was struck by someone, treated very badly by a member of the Yeomanry, and they were the ones who charged into the meeting. She describes how that happened and how other people around her were basically hit and injured by the action of the Yeomanry and the cavalry. And it took her several days, if not weeks, to recover from the experience.

> "She describes how other people around her were hit and injured by the yeomanry"

Record-keeping at Westminster dates back as far as 1497 and includes bills, motions and more from both the House of Commons and House of Lords

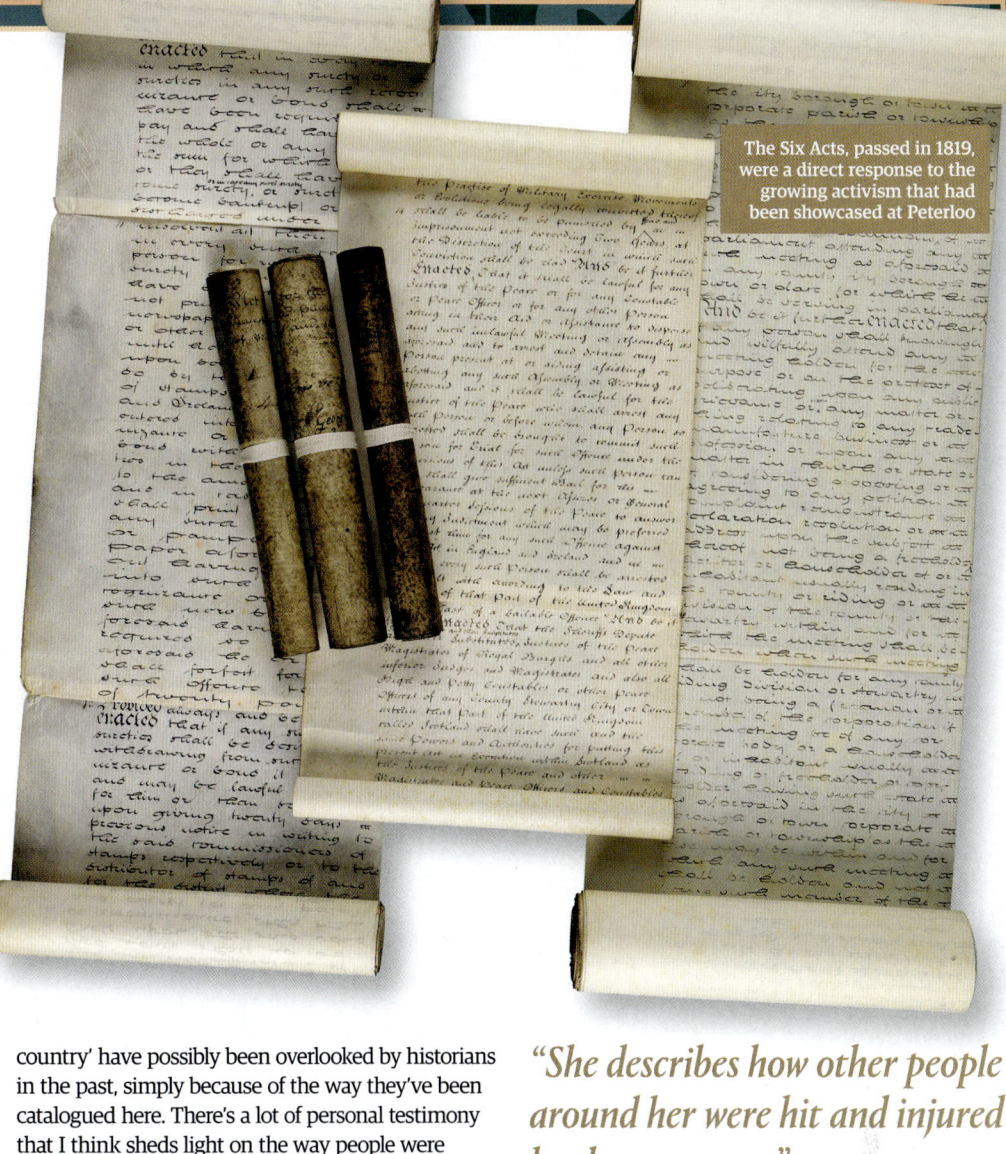

67

POLITICS & POWER

A Permanent Memorial

The Peterloo Massacre Campaign held a number of events to bring more attention to Peterloo, such as this gathering with protestors carrying the names of the 1819 victims

PAUL FITZGERALD
Peterloo Massacre Campaign chairman

Artist Jeremy Deller unveils plans for his Peterloo memorial

How did the campaign for a permanent memorial to the victims of the Peterloo Massacre get started?
I'm a professional political cartoonist and was drawing a cartoon that used Tiananmen Square as a metaphor about the rise of capitalism and consumerism in China and kept getting this weird feeling that it reminded me of something... but what?

Then the penny dropped. It's Peterloo. I very quickly began asking why Manchester has no memorial to an event that changed Britain and the world. We know why the regime in China wouldn't commemorate Tiananmen, but what excuse did my home city have?

About the same time some delegates at the Labour Party annual conference, which was being held very near the site of the massacre, were wandering about in a break, seeing if they could find any indicators of what happened there, and couldn't. We ended up joining forces with them after our launch.

What have been the biggest challenges to getting approval for the memorial?
It was a pretty open door in terms of the basic yes to the idea. The really big challenge was to push the council to make sure there was a genuine and of course profoundly appropriate democratic input into what the design should consist of, and that was a nightmare of anger and frustration. They exerted a really shocking level of control over it, and despite our efforts to pressure them, they revealed the design and held a token consultation in late 2018, too late for any serious objections or revisions. Since then we've all been drowning in bitter irony at how undemocratic the process of choosing a memorial to democracy has been. It's all very telling, eh?

How was the final design concept for the memorial decided upon?
We pushed hard for an open design competition, but ultimately it would seem very few people in the council hierarchy had a yes or no say about artist Jeremy Deller's design. We did, however, manage to get our 'RIP' criteria for the memorial incorporated into the process: Respectful, Informative and Permanent/Prominent, and I think those have been met. But it seemed to take a formal Freedom of Information demand to pry that inner door open.

How well-known are the events of Peterloo to the people of Manchester?
Until recently, it was the norm not to know about it in the city. There really has been a 200-year whitewashing of its memory. We hope our persistence over the years has helped combat that and that Mike Leigh's film does the same.

You've just published a graphic novel about Peterloo. What can you tell us about that project?
Yeah, it's all come round in a circle regarding my 'day job'! Myself, Eva Schlunke and historian Professor Robert Poole recently finished *Peterloo: Witnesses to a Massacre*. We deeply hope it'll prove a very accessible and populist way for people to find out more. Just researching it was an amazing experience.

Much of the text is actually from reporting and government correspondence from the day. Why did you choose this approach?
Everything in it, in a white narrative or speech bubble, is simply 100 per cent accurate and taken from the huge range of sources that exist; courtroom transcripts, spy's reports, journals, diaries and so on. They alone, without the images, make for an astonishing and moving read, with deeply contrasting attitudes from the huge range of characters. We think this may be the world's first 'verbatim' graphic novel!

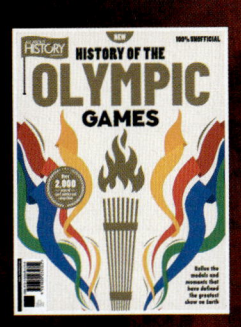

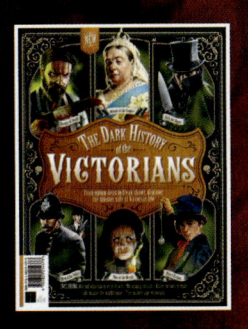

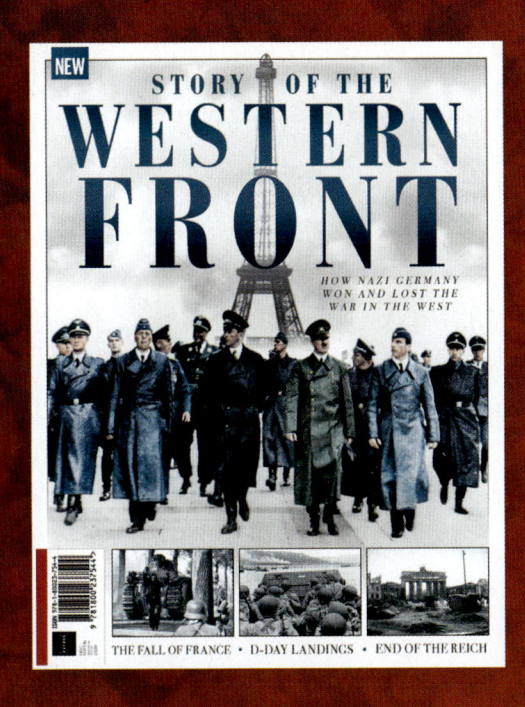

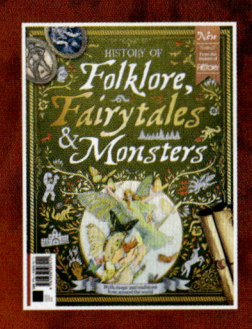

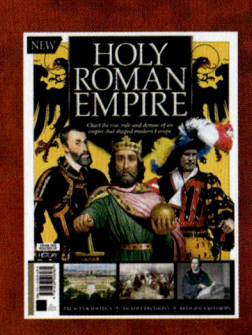

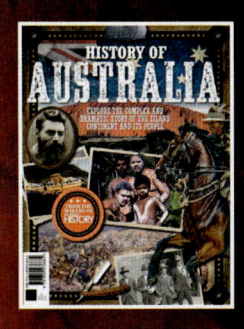

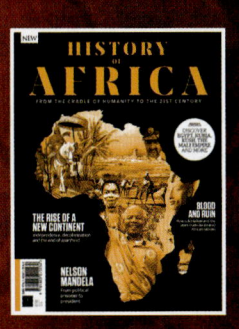

STEP BACK IN TIME WITH OUR HISTORY TITLES

Immerse yourself in a world of emperors, pioneers, conquerors and legends and discover the events that shaped humankind

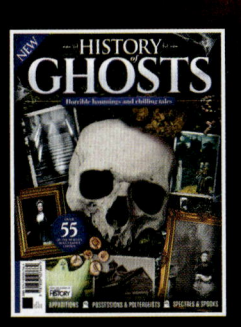

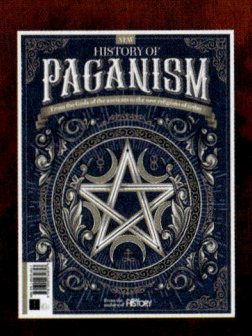

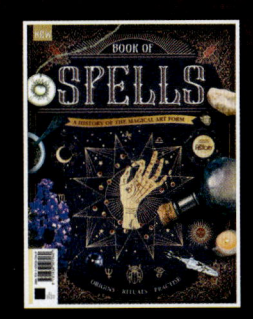

Follow us on Instagram @futurebookazines

www.magazinesdirect.com/history

Magazines, back issues & bookazines.

POLITICS & POWER

By the time American forces repelled the British assault on New Orleans, peace had been declared. However, news of it had not reached America

BRITAIN AT WAR

During the first half of the Regency era, Britain found itself almost constantly at war. Unsurprisingly, the impact on the nation was enormous

WRITTEN BY **CATHERINE CURZON**

When the Prince Regent took up the reins of power in 1811, the United Kingdom had been embroiled in the Napoleonic Wars for eight years. The country was tired, its resources stretched and with no obvious end in sight, there was little hope of respite.

But then things got even worse – on 18 June 1812, the United States declared war on the United Kingdom and its allies. Tensions had been rising in the former colony for years, rooted in disagreements over territorial expansion and the UK's support for Tecumseh's confederacy, which aimed to prevent settlers from colonising Native American territory in the Old Northwest. When

The Treaty of Ghent, signed on Christmas Eve, 1814, ended the War of 1812. News, however, travelled slow

POLITICS & POWER

the Royal Navy began increasing restrictions on American trade with the French, things became even more tense. The House and Senate voted to declare war and though the British responded with a list of the concessions they were willing to make to avoid conflict, this communication did not reach America until late July. By that time, the war had begun.

As the Royal Navy blockaded trade, British soldiers and colonial militia loyal to the King joined forces to defeat repeated American invasions of Upper Canada. The situation escalated to a new level when Napoleon abdicated in April 1814, thus freeing up British ships that could then sail for the US, where they made the blockade ironclad. With its trade completely crippled, the American economy was driven into the ground. Yet while this may seem like a victory, the blockade had a devastating impact on the British economy too, which had suddenly found all its trade with the US cut off.

With both sides tired of conflict, peace negotiations began in Ghent in August 1814, just as British forces captured Washington, while American victories in Baltimore and Plattsburgh the following month put an end to the war in the north. In Belgium, the British and American delegates signed the Treaty of Ghent on 24 December 1814, which ended the war and restored things to how they had been before the first shots were fired, with Great Britain agreeing to relinquish its interests in the Northwest Territory.

"The Spanish and Portuguese revolted, with Britain lending its might to what became the Peninsular War"

However, though the war was officially over as far as the delegates were concerned, it took weeks for the news to get to the US. During this period, one of the final acts of the war occurred in January 1815, when American troops led by Andrew Jackson held New Orleans against an attack by the British. One month later, President James Madison signed and ratified the Treaty of Ghent, thus bringing peace to the United States.

Although the war against America was over, the one against Napoleon was not. The Napoleonic Wars began in 1803 and were fought between the armies of the French Republic and a changing cast of European coalitions. The long, exhausting conflict came out of the French Revolutionary Wars as Napoleon sought to expand French influence in Europe in the wake of the Revolution and began on 18 May 1803, when Britain and the Third Coalition declared war against France. France, however, defeated the Russo-Austrian army at Austerlitz, leading to the Fourth Coalition, under which Napoleon scored more decisive victories, this time over Prussia and Russia, leading to an unsettled period of peace.

However, in 1809 Austria led the Fifth Coalition against Napoleon but after claiming what seemed like a decisive victory, were soon defeated. With Portugal Britain's only remaining ally in Europe, as it defied Napoleon's blockade on trade with Great Britain, Napoleon invaded Portugal and closed the ports to British ships, aiming to bring Britain to its knees economically. However, Napoleon's actions alarmed his Spanish allies and when he replaced the Spanish royal family with his own kin and installed his brother as King of Spain, they were tested to their limits. Instead, the Spanish and Portuguese revolted, with Britain lending its might to what became the Peninsular War.

Napoleon underestimated the ferocity with which the Portuguese and Spanish would fight for their lands. He ordered his troops to move swiftly to crush the rebellion but instead met with defeat at Bailén in July 1808, when 12,000 of his soldiers surrendered. This was a major setback for France and led to the rebels claiming back much of Iberia. It was the first open-field defeat for the Napoleonic army and when the defeated French general, Pierre Dupont, handed his sword to Spain's General Castaños, he commended his foe on being the first person to defeat him in innumerable battles. Castaños replied that the victory was far more remarkable for another reason: it was the first battle that he had ever fought.

Only now did the Spanish appeal to the British for help and it came in the shape of 14,000 troops under the command of the future Duke

The French defeat at Bailén, early in the Peninsular War, was Napoleon's first open-field defeat. It had not been the expected outcome

Napoleon's decision to install his brother, Joseph, as King of Spain in 1808 proved disastrous. He abdicated in 1813

of Wellington. Though the French massively outnumbered the British, they had reckoned without the Iberian insurgents, who led raids and ambushes on French supply lines and garrisons that hobbled them. By 1812, 200,000 of the 350,000 French soldiers in Iberia were protecting supply lines rather than fighting. Constantly frustrated by what he called the "Spanish ulcer", Napoleon had not expected the revolt in Iberia to rumble on, but rumble on it did. Eventually, in 1812, he withdrew many troops to take part in his catastrophic invasion of Russia, which led to the near complete destruction of his Grande Armée. Now the British and Iberian forces took advantage and pushed forward, liberating city after city and pushing the French into retreat over the Pyrenees. Following the decisive Battle of Vitoria on 21 June 1813, Joseph Bonaparte abdicated the throne of Spain, but Wellington wasn't done. He led his army into Southern France, bringing the fight into the heart of Napoleon's empire.

With the defeat in Russia, the Sixth Coalition of the United Kingdom, Austria, Prussia, Sweden and Russia joined forces for what they hoped would be the endgame in this long conflict. With the French unable to regroup after its defeat in Russia, they were routed at the Battle of Leipzig in October 1813, leaving what was left of Napoleon's Grande Armée in tatters. With little defence remaining, Coalition troops invaded France, capturing Paris in March 1814. Finally defeated, Napoleon abdicated and was exiled to Elba, where he remained until

The Congress of Vienna
With Napoleon's defeat, it was time to redraw Europe

When the Congress of Vienna met for a series of negotiations in 1814 and 1815, its aim was to agree a new layout of the European political and constitutional landscape, which would bring long-term peace to Europe.

Under the chairmanship of Austria's Klemens von Metternich, the Congress would not simply restore the status quo but would instead redraw the size of the most powerful nations in order to ensure that they were balanced and therefore would not seek conflict. The major powers – Austria, United Kingdom, Russia and Prussia – would then steer the smaller powers to ensure peace prevailed. Represented by foreign minister and master negotiator, Talleyrand, France was compelled to surrender all its recent territorial conquests but hoped soon to be back to its place at the table among the major powers.

The Final Act of the Congress of Vienna was signed on 9 June, redrawing significant parts of the previous landscape of Europe. Though the conclusions of the Congress continue to attract praise and criticism, it prevented another major war for almost a century and was used by the British as a model for the Paris Peace Conference of 1919, proving how far its influence reached.

The Final Act of the Congress of Vienna aimed to prevent conflict

Napoleon's attempted invasion of Russia proved catastrophic. He barely escaped capture by Russian forces as he retreated from Moscow

his escape the following February. After the famed Hundred Days, the armies of the Seventh Coalition met Napoleon's forces on the battlefield at Waterloo, ending his reign for good.

The wars had a dramatic impact on the UK, which had seen its people taxed to a seemingly endless degree to meet the costs of the conflicts. It is estimated more than 300,000 Britons died in the Napoleonic Wars and the state spent millions on the conflict, leading to strained economic circumstances. Unemployment soared and with it hunger, poverty and disease. Though the ultimate victory over Napoleon at Waterloo was celebrated in fine style across the country, as people were able to briefly forget what the cost of that victory had been, life was soon back to normal and with it came renewed protests and calls for action.

Though the wars of the Regency era may seem a long way from the ballrooms of *Bridgerton*, there were few who weren't touched by them one way or another. In those years, from America to Europe, the world changed forever and while the government and the Prince Regent toasted their victory, for those who had struggled with taxation, hunger, poverty and loss, there was little to celebrate. Victory had come at an enormous cost not only to the United Kingdom, but to those countries who had formed coalitions and alliances to bring down Napoleon, and the shockwaves would be felt for a very long time to come.

POLITICS & POWER

BATTLE OF WATERLOO

WATERLOO, BELGIUM 18 JUNE 1815

NAPOLEON'S BODYGUARD
Protecting Napoleon during the battle were his Old Guard - elite veterans of the Imperial Guard that he handpicked based on their combat experience. One of the most common traits was above average height, meaning that they towered over many other units on the battlefield.

The bloody culmination of the Waterloo Campaign, the Battle of Waterloo was one of the most explosive of the 19th century, with a British-led allied army under the command of Arthur Wellesley, the Duke of Wellington, defeating a French army under the command of Napoleon Bonaparte and ending the latter's 100-day reign as emperor of France.

The war had begun after Napoleon I returned from exile on Elba (an island off Tuscany) to Paris on 20 March 1815. This set into motion a chain of events that would see Napoleon reclaim his position as emperor, the Congress of Vienna declare him an outlaw and the Seventh Coalition pledge to field a large army to bring his rule to an end.

With hundreds of thousands of soldiers drafted to take Napoleon down, it was only a matter of time before blood was spilt - something that occurred two days prior to Waterloo when Napoleon struck at the Prussian army before it could join up with Wellington's on 16 June.

The French ruler did this by splitting his army into three groups, with two dedicated to the Prussians. The following exchange was the Battle of Ligny and saw Napoleon defeat the Prussians by causing their centre to collapse under repeated French assaults. While the Prussians lost men, they were not routed however and - as we shall see - were disastrously left to retreat uninterrupted, with only a cursory French force giving chase.

On the same day as the Battle of Ligny, Napoleon's army's remaining left flank had been engaged with some of Wellington's forces at Quatre Bras, where they had attempted unsuccessfully to overrun the Prince of Orange's position. With the Prussians apparently defeated, Napoleon turned his attention on Quatre Bras, reaching the area the following day. By this point, however, it was too late, as Quatre Bras had been abandoned by both sides; Wellington could not hold it without the Prussians. After catching up with his left flank commander, Marshal Michel Ney, who was pursuing a retreating Wellington towards Waterloo, Napoleon ordered his right flank commander, Marshal Emmanuel de Grouchy, to see off the Prussians more definitively.

By this time, with Napoleon issuing the order late on the afternoon of 17 June, the Prussians had already made significant ground and regrouped at the town of Wavre - a position from which they could easily rejoin Wellington at Waterloo - and Marshal Grouchy was unsuccessful in catching them. Despite eventually defeating a solitary Prussian Corps at Wavre on 18 June, by this time the Battle of Waterloo was in full swing and Grouchy was unable to take part.

After Napoleon had issued the order to Marshal Grouchy he continued to hunt down Wellington with his remaining forces before making camp south-west of Wellington's position at Waterloo. The scene was now set for the Battle of Waterloo the next day (18 June), which resulted in a famous victory for the Duke of Wellington and a final defeat for Emperor Napoleon.

As a consequence of Napoleon's loss at Waterloo, the French monarchy was restored, with King Louis XVIII regaining the throne on 8 July 1815, while the emperor himself was banished to the volcanic island of Saint Helena in the Atlantic Ocean. Napoleon would live on Saint Helena for a further six years, before passing away in May 1821.

BATTLE OF WATERLOO

SCOTS GREYS
The charge of the Royal Scots Greys at Waterloo became symbolic of the courage demonstrated by Coalition forces in the face of the might of Napoleon's army. Their charge famously repelled a key French advance, caused the complete destruction of a large French infantry column and led to the capture of Napoleon's 45th Regiment of the Line's eagle standard.

SEVENTH COALITION
While the primary antagonists of the Battle of Waterloo were the UK and France, a host of other nations played a part, joining with the British to form a coalition against the new emperor of France. These included the Netherlands, Hanover, Nassau, Bavaria and Prussia – the latter contributing most significantly.

HEAVY LOSSES
While Waterloo was not a medieval meat-grinder of a battle, with tactics very firmly on display, it still had a huge casualty list. Of Napoleon's 72,000 troops, around 25,000 were killed outright or wounded, 8,000 were taken prisoner and 15,000 went missing. The total for Wellington and his allies' soldiers killed, wounded or missing came to around 24,000.

POLITICS & POWER

Seventh Coalition

TROOPS 118,000
CAVALRY 11,000
CANNONS 150

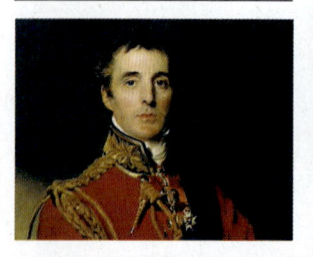

DUKE OF WELLINGTON
Leader
Rising to prominence in the Napoleonic Wars, Arthur Wellesley remained commander-in-chief of the British Army until his death in 1852.
Strengths Very confident and energetic leader.
Weakness Not the most tactically astute of generals.

INFANTRY
Important Unit
Among the best on the planet, the infantry dug in deep at Waterloo to deny many French cavalry charges.
Strength Versatile troops that could fight at close range.
Weaknesses Easily outflanked by cavalry and vulnerable to cannons.

CANNON
Key weapon
Very destructive, the Coalition's artillery helped slow the French forces and break up their lines.
Strengths Cannons had excellent range and could do a lot of damage.
Weaknesses Needed supporting troops for protection as fairly fragile under fire and few in number.

01 FIRST FORAY
Between 10 and 11.30am on 18 June the Battle of Waterloo began with a French attack on a Coalition position at Hougoumont, a large farmhouse that served as a tactical outpost. This fighting was low key at first with few troops from each side engaged, but by the early afternoon it had become a bloody epicentre for much of the fighting, with the Coalition forces holding out against numerous French assaults.

02 GRANDE BATTERIE
Around midday Napoleon ordered his grande batterie of 80 cannons to open fire upon Wellington's position. The cannons caused many casualties in Wellington's cavalry, opening a potential weak point in the defending lines.

10 FRENCH ARMY RETREATS
With the French left, right and centre now disintegrating, the only cohesive force left available to Napoleon were two battalions of his Old Guard. Despite hoping to rally his remaining troops behind them, the strength of the Coalition's forces left this untenable, and all Napoleon could do was order a retreat. His exit was covered by the Old Guard, many of whom died holding back the Coalition's advance.

03 FRENCH INFANTRY ATTACK
After the Coalition's lines had been weakened, Napoleon began his attack proper, with numerous infantry corps advancing. The initial fighting went the way of the French, with the left's infantry pressing Wellington's forces back. However, just when it looked like Napoleon would make a decisive break, he was informed that Prussian troops were fast approaching. He tried to send word to Marshal Grouchy to engage with them, but his commander was in Wavre.

04 BRITISH HEAVY CAVALRY ATTACK
Seeing their infantry was about to buckle, Wellington's First and Second Brigade of heavy cavalry charged and smashed into the French infantry. By the time they reached the bottom of the hill, they had completely halted the infantry's advance. In doing so, however, they had left themselves exposed and without backup.

BATTLE OF WATERLOO

09 PLANCENOIT RECAPTURED
The Prussian army retook Plancenoit and targeted Napoleon's right flank, giving Wellington the upper hand. The Old Guard who had been supporting the French position at Plancenoit beat a hasty retreat.

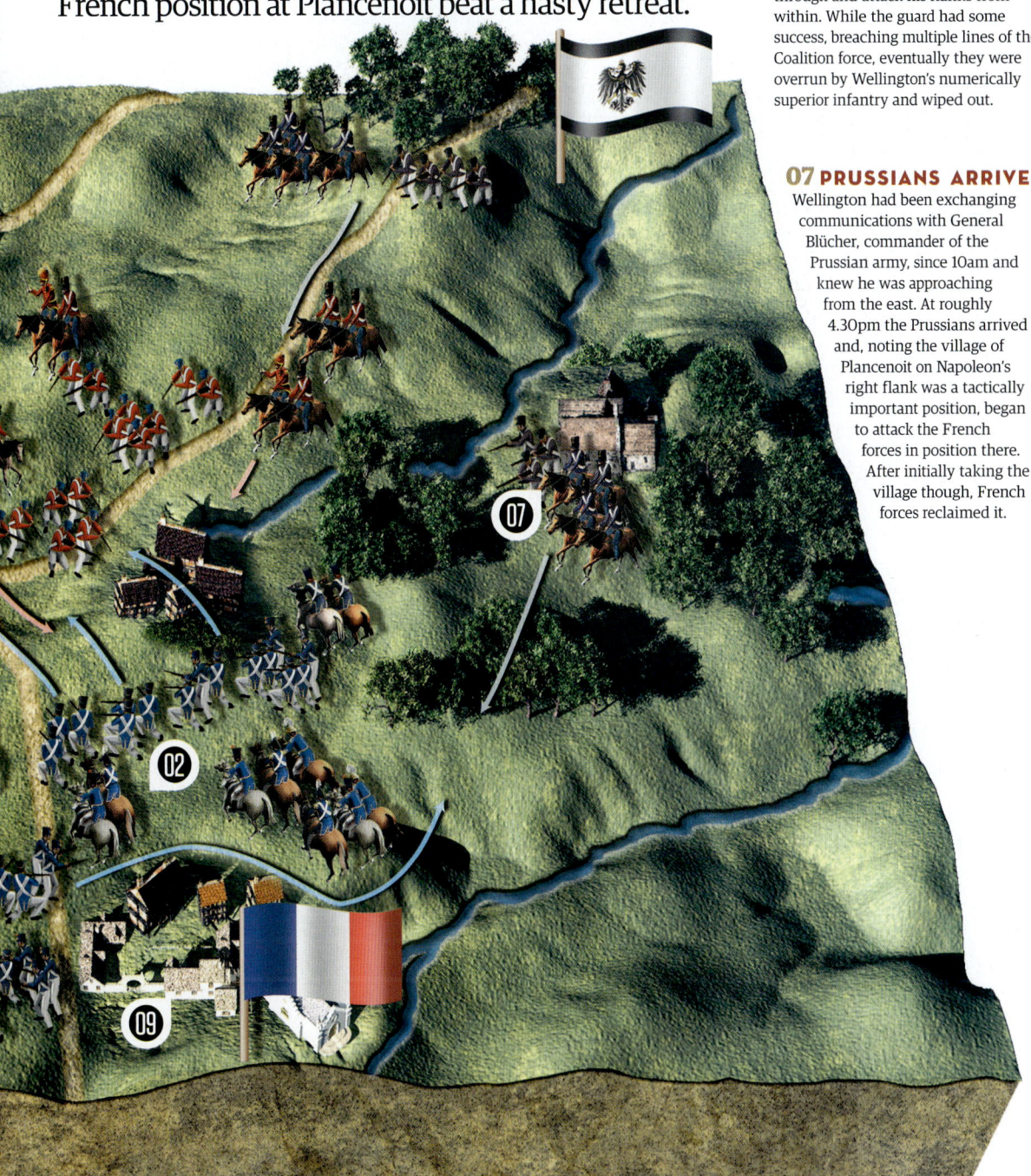

08 IMPERIAL GUARD ATTACKS WELLINGTON
With his forces temporarily holding off the Prussians at Plancenoit, Napoleon went on one last major offensive. He sent the supposedly undefeatable Imperial Guard into Wellington's army's centre in an attempt to break through and attack his flanks from within. While the guard had some success, breaching multiple lines of the Coalition force, eventually they were overrun by Wellington's numerically superior infantry and wiped out.

07 PRUSSIANS ARRIVE
Wellington had been exchanging communications with General Blücher, commander of the Prussian army, since 10am and knew he was approaching from the east. At roughly 4.30pm the Prussians arrived and, noting the village of Plancenoit on Napoleon's right flank was a tactically important position, began to attack the French forces in position there. After initially taking the village though, French forces reclaimed it.

France
TROOPS 72,000
CAVALRY 14,000
CANNONS 250

NAPOLEON BONAPARTE
Leader
Emperor Bonaparte became famous for his tactical genius, enabling him to take over much of central Europe.
Strengths A savvy strategist with plenty of battle experience.
Weaknesses Erratic; he took a detached approach to fighting.

CAVALRY
Important Unit
French light cavalry was considered the best of its kind in the world and played a large part in holding off the Coalition's heavy cavalry charges.
Strength Fast, agile units capable of easily outflanking the enemy.
Weakness Direct cavalry charges rely on surprise to be most effective.

MUSKET
Key weapon
The musket was wielded by Napoleon's Old Guard with deadly accuracy, picking off large numbers of Coalition soldiers at Waterloo.
Strength Excellent medium-range stopping power.
Weaknesses Slow to reload and also poor in hand-to-hand combat.

05 NAPOLEON COUNTERS
With the Coalition's heavy cavalry now facing squares of French infantry to the front and with no support, Napoleon ordered a counterattack, dispatching his cuirassier and lancer regiments from his own cavalry division. A massive central battle ensued, with cavalry, infantry and artillery all involved. While Napoleon's cavalry regiments took out much of the Coalition's heavy cavalry, they could not wipe them out. Napoleon also dispatched troops to intercept the Prussians.

06 STALEMATE
At the heart of the battle, Coalition and French squares then undertook a series of exchanges. All the while cannon and musket fire continued to rain down from all sides and, aside from one more combined arms assault by the French on the centre-right of Wellington's lines, a general mêlée ensued, with each side seeing their numbers steadily chipped away.

POLITICS & POWER

Granville Sharp: Civil rights pioneer

Granville Sharp was one of the earliest abolitionists in Britain and fought a successful legal case in the 1760s to release a badly beaten young Barbadian from his abusive master. In 1772 he won another decisive victory on the road to abolition, when he successfully argued in court that the concept of slavery had no basis in English law – therefore no man who set foot in England could be a slave.

Despite having common law on his side, his legal opponents were financed by wealthy plantation owners in the Caribbean, and a number of influential politicians owned plantations or had shares in the trade.

A 1783 case gave him an opportunity to bring the callousness of the slave trade to public attention. It was a simple insurance hearing – a percentage of slave ship Zong's cargo had been jettisoned overboard and, as such, the ship's owners were entitled to compensation. Zong had wandered off course and water supplies were dwindling, so 132 kidnapped Africans has been thrown overboard by the crew in order to ensure the remainder would survive.

The judge rejected the compensation claims and although no crew were prosecuted, the 'Zong Massacre' horrified many who had otherwise never given the business a second thought at all.

The Slave Ship by JMW Turner, 1840, inspired by an account of the Zong Massacre

The wife of a Scottish plantation owner walks on her estate on either Carriacou or Granada; their 'favourite slave' Didi walks behind them, 1810s

THE WAR ON SLAVERY

Abolition was born with the Quakers and religious non-conformists, but over five decades, freedom was won by the slaves themselves

WRITTEN BY **JAMES HOARE**

Britain's slave trade may have been birthed by the Stuarts, but it was under the Georgians that it grew in scale to match the booming cotton, tobacco and sugar cane industries in Britain's colonies. Over the 1780s - the reign of George III - more than 300,000 kidnapped Africans left their homes in chains on board British ships. Only 276,100 arrived, the rest dying of disease, dehydration, malnutrition or abuse during the torturous crossing.

The first organised resistance came from Quakers. Anti-slavery tracts by the American Quaker Anthony Benezet were distributed across the English-speaking world and in Britain John Wesley took up the cause, galvanising his fledgling Methodist church as a force for abolition.

In 1786, three powerful forces were drawn together. A young Cambridge graduate and Anglican deacon called Thomas Clarkson won a prize for his *An Essay on the Slavery and Commerce of the Human Species*, and captured the imagination of Yorkshire MP William Wilberforce. The two agreed to work together, while the Quakers provided their well-oiled machine, printing and distributing Clarkson's text.

Quakers also made up nine of the 13 founding members of the Society for Effecting the Abolition of the Slave Trade, which found Christians - regardless of denomination - to be its core base, although women and the working class became increasingly sympathetic to the emotional arguments.

While the American Revolution of 1775 had emboldened the abolitionists, the French Revolution of 1789 knocked the wind from their sails. Their arguments - carrying with them the whiff of revolutionary ideals - were treated with suspicion across the 1790s, while the bloody slave uprising on the French colony of St Domingue (Haiti) between 1791 and 1804 appeared to validate those who cautioned against sparing the whip. This situation was made worse by slave revolts in British-held Jamaica, Grenada, St Vincent and St Lucia, and the disastrous attempt by Britain to invade St Domingue.

Peace with France and, more crucially, Napoleon Bonaparte's reintroduction of slavery to the French Empire, gave Wilberforce and Clarkson the ammunition they needed. In May 1806, the Foreign Slave Trade Act was passed banning British subjects from transporting slaves to foreign powers - aimed at the French, it didn't affect British colonies and made it through the usually obstructive Lords. In the general election of September 1806, slavery emerged as a major campaign issue.

The official emblem of the Anti-Slavery Society, designed by Josiah Wedgwood in 1795

Despite the new government holding only a thin majority, the Slave Trade Act 1807 was passed overwhelmingly, prohibiting the trade in the British Empire. Slavery itself endured, but to the abolitionists it appeared as though it might simply fade away of its own accord.

In 1816, during the Regency, a slave revolt in Barbados could well have hit public opinion with all the visceral fury of St Domingue, but the climate had changed completely. Missionary work in the Caribbean had transformed most of the slaves from unknowable 'savages' in the eyes of white Britons to civilised Christians, while first-hand accounts from freed slaves gave them a feel for the suffering that was being endured. In this, Methodist and Baptist churches acted as direct lines of communication and solidarity between two sets of brethren thousands of miles apart.

It was a revolt in Demerara (Guyana) that marked the beginning of the end. Arguably the harshest and most repressive regime in the empire, the missionary John Smith arrived in 1817. When the slaves rose up in 1823, the reaction was brutal. As punishment for the revolt, which killed three white settlers, 250 black slaves were killed. Smith was tried for agitation. He died in jail before his death sentence could be carried out.

Society was scandalised, and Wilberforce and Clarkson took up the cause of the 'Demerara Martyr'. However, they now had another factor on their side: slavery was no longer just immoral, it was uneconomic and cheaper sugar was available from elsewhere. Now the British public were being asked by powerful vested interests to pay more and in doing so subsidise a cruel and exploitative system, the case for slavery was rapidly collapsing.

In 1831 there was a large-scale revolt on Jamaica led by the Baptist preacher Sam Sharpe. An estimated 60,000 rose up and 14 white people were killed - as with Demerara, the retaliation was disproportionate. 540 slaves were killed and the powerful image of Sharpe echoed the righteousness of the Demerara Martyr.

The Slavery Abolition Act 1833 was a slow-moving reform, initially releasing only those under six years old. The rest remained bound to their masters for six years as unpaid 'apprentices'. In addition, slave owners were to be paid vast sums in compensation from a pool of £20 million. For the House of Lords, who remained closely linked to the planters, it was a sign that all they had left was the negotiation of a surrender that wouldn't leave them too out of pocket. The survival of the system was no longer an option.

CULTURE & KNOWLEDGE

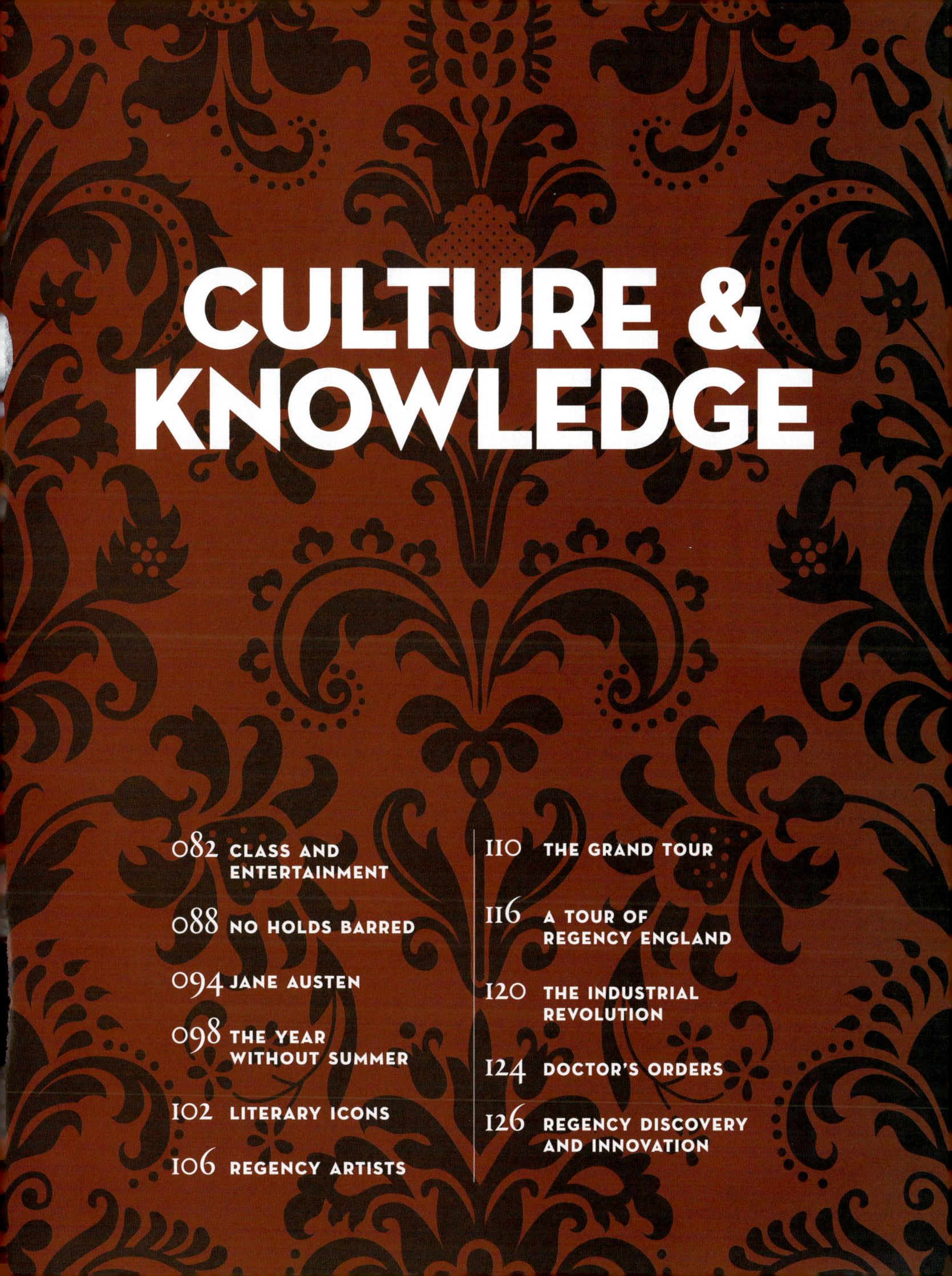

082 CLASS AND ENTERTAINMENT

088 NO HOLDS BARRED

094 JANE AUSTEN

098 THE YEAR WITHOUT SUMMER

102 LITERARY ICONS

106 REGENCY ARTISTS

110 THE GRAND TOUR

116 A TOUR OF REGENCY ENGLAND

120 THE INDUSTRIAL REVOLUTION

124 DOCTOR'S ORDERS

126 REGENCY DISCOVERY AND INNOVATION

Before parliamentary reform, artists like William Hogarth captured the chaos and corruption of British elections

In the Georgian world, life for the upper classes was all about power, brilliance and privilege

CLASS AND ENTERTAINMENT

Georgian Britain was a world of contrasts. Yet from the richest to the poorest, everyone loved having a good time

WRITTEN BY **CATHERINE CURZON**

In the heady world of the Georgians, Great Britain's class system – lauded by some, decried by others – had become a somewhat fluid concept. The world was changing at a rapid rate for rich and poor alike, as modernisation swept across the kingdom. Britain's ancient feudal system had been swept aside by the English Civil War. Where once there had been an unchallenged, all-powerful aristocracy, there was now a new class. This was a rising group of wealthy entrepreneurs and gentry, the nouveau riche whose wealth came not from their dynastic history, but industry and enterprise.

Once the upper classes had been the purview of those who owned the most land but as the century progressed, the Industrial Revolution saw the social landscape change, allowing for more social mobility. The upper classes were being infiltrated by those who might not have been born to land-owning families, but were growing wealthy through manufacturing and trade, with rich new opportunities created by the expanding British empire. Beneath them a new middle class emerged too, made up of those educated employees who filled the roles that existed between business owners and workers. There were the clerks and professionals, those with enterprise and ambition who hoped to break into the upper class one day too.

Though the nouveau riche was flourishing, the working class remained subdued. All this ambition and social climbing relied on the industry of workers. For those at the bottom, life was hard. After all, the rising middle class could hardly extend their fortune to their workers, or who knew where it might end? Electoral reforms might benefit the middle classes and disenfranchise the upper class, but for the working class, their moment of suffrage was a long time coming.

Life for the rich was a constant round of visits, business and entertainment. Georgians loved to show off their wealth!

CULTURE & KNOWLEDGE

The upper class life

In work as well as play, life for upper class Georgians was governed by protocol, rank and privilege

As the Georgian era dawned over Great Britain, the once-established order was in a state of flux. For centuries, wealth had been equated to land and to enjoy a place in the rarified upper class, you needed to possess a great deal of land indeed. At the top of the pile sat the monarchy and beneath that, the aristocracy and peerage, whose family names could be traced back through the generations and centuries of royal favour.

Beneath them was the landed gentry, landlords who owned estates that financed their lifestyles. These were educated men, alumni of famous private schools who followed in the footsteps of their forefathers. They sat in parliament, representing the seats that their ancestors had before them, and their careers were drawn from traditional, respectable worlds such as government, the law or the military.

The 18th century upper classes lived in a world of inherited wealth and privilege where titles, property and money passed down from one generation to the next. Eldest children, usually but not always male, were destined to become the head of the family in their turn, just as they had for generations. For those lucky enough to be courtiers, meanwhile, the atmosphere was rarified indeed. These individuals made their lives at the heart of the royal circle, usually serving in roles that assisted the monarch or the running of the household and the pickings could be rich.

Naturally, for men and women the experience was very different. The eldest son of a family was trained to take his father's place, while the younger would be expected to go into a respectable profession. Their daughters, however, had no such prospects. Their education was traditionally limited to the skills that would make them an attractive proposition to would-be suitors. Male and female alike learned good manners and etiquette, but while young men might be sent overseas on a Grand Tour, their sisters were learning to dance and sing, to paint and play instruments, and generally, with an eye to their futures, to 'sparkle'. Only when they were ready were they presented at court, officially introduced to the queen in a ceremony that essentially told the world these young ladies were ripe for marriage.

Of course, some women broke away from the accepted order, but they were few and far between. In the upper classes of the 18th century, progress was a rarely heard word.

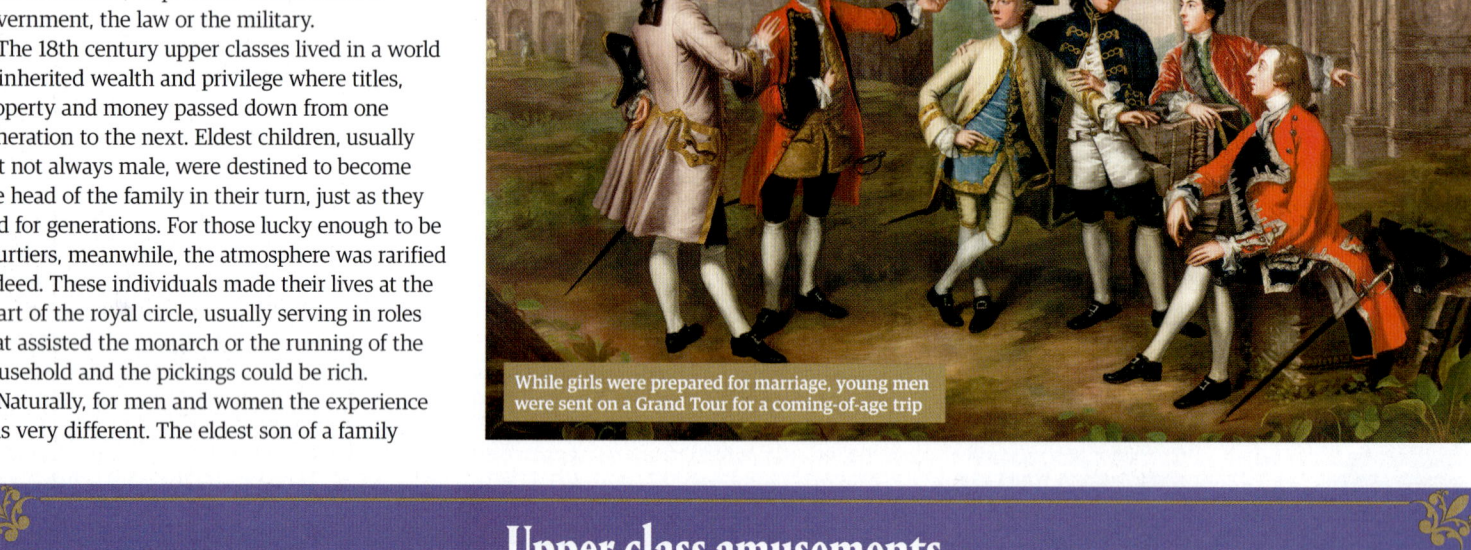

While girls were prepared for marriage, young men were sent on a Grand Tour for a coming-of-age trip

Upper class amusements

Horse racing
Horse racing in Georgian Britain was a chance to network. Royals could be charmed, careers progressed. In the winner's enclosure, monarchs could often be glimpsed celebrating the victory of their own horses.

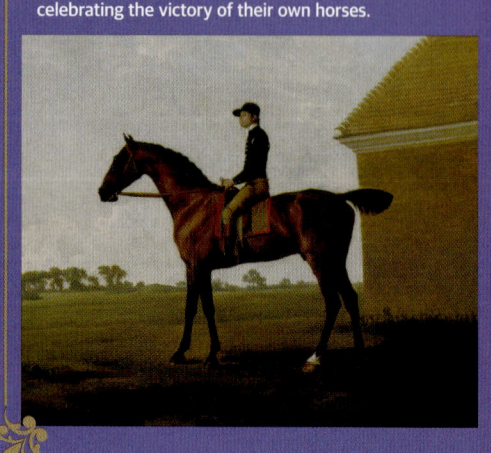

Hunting in the country
Hunting was particularly popular with 18th century men. As well as the thrill of the chase, a hunt meet was a chance to oil the wheels of business too.

The pleasure gardens
No Georgian night on the town was complete without a visit to the Pleasure Gardens. Here one could stroll along lamplit avenues, enjoy a meal and entertainment, or marvel at breathtaking landscapes.

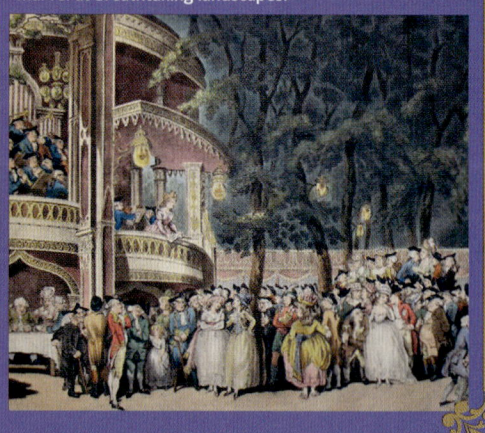

A day in the life of the upper classes

Run the household

After taking breakfast with her children, the lady of the house would spend some time with her housekeeper, addressing matters regarding the running of the house and any particularly requirements or concerns. For younger ladies, this was time for education and self-improvement, geared towards following their mother into this vital domestic role. As married ladies and their housekeepers conversed, their daughters undertook lessons that were crafted to create the perfect model of a future bride. From learning languages to music lessons and even prayer to ensure just the right amount of piety, self-improvement was the name of the game. After all, there were a lot of marriageable young ladies in the world, so it was important to stand out!

Ladies were expected to be accomplished in the feminine arts, a ready-made ornament for their households

Dress for dinner

After luncheon, or nuncheon, if a lady had an important engagement in the evening, it wouldn't be at all strange for her to spend the entire afternoon preparing for the night to come. After a suitable period of rest, it was time to be dressed and primped ready to face the public. In the era of enormous panniers and even bigger hair, the richest ladies would be attended by a whole entourage of dressers and coiffeurs, dedicated to creating the perfect picture of wealthy femininity. The most elaborate hairdos would be held up by wooden or wire structures, stuffed with padding and powder, and decorated with elaborate ornamentation that could last for days on end!

Dressing for a formal evening was a serious affair. It could easily take hours and a whole team of attendants

Enjoy a feast with friends

A formal dinner would begin in the early evening and should be expected to last for several hours. These dinners were elaborate and highly regimented affairs, intended to cement social standing and position. Seating plans were strictly adhered to and reflected the status of the guests, subtly conveying a wealth of social messages to the attendees. After dinner, the women retired to the drawing room together and left the men alone in the dining room to discuss business and matters that were, supposedly, far too weighty for feminine minds to comprehend! It was a chance for fathers to sing the praises of their daughters, of course, should any of the men present have eligible sons looking for a bride.

Formal dinners were long affairs and the finest foods were served to show off the bountiful wealth of the host

Take in a show at the theatre

Though a trip to the theatre wouldn't be a nightly occurrence, for an upper class family it was certainly a regular event. This was a pastime that all classes could share, though their experiences would be very different indeed. In the early Georgian era, the most wealthy attendees could pay a surcharge to sit on the stage itself, which allowed them to show off their finery to an audience that might well contain some of their contemporaries or would-be suitors. The Georgian kings and their families regularly attended the theatre, and the upper classes might use this as an opportunity to properly show their deference and respect to the monarch, not to mention one-up their rivals and peers!

The rich could rub shoulders with royalty at the theatre and watch legends like Garrick and Mrs Siddons perform!

CULTURE & KNOWLEDGE

Lower class life

For lower class Georgians life could be hard, but there was still room for fun

To be working class in 18th century society didn't necessarily mean to be poor, but whether living in the rookery or scraping a living in the factories, it was far from glamorous.

In a country with a swiftly rising population, economic times could be hard and lower class Georgians felt this more than ever. The seams of the cities of England seemed stretched to bursting and for those at the bottom of the heap, this meant they were forced into the glowering rookeries, tightly packed housing where deprivation was the norm. Education was the preserve of a fortunate few indeed and often provided by the church, but in a world where money was scarce, working was the only option if you didn't want to starve.

Work was heavy and as the century advanced, men, women and children alike sought employment in factories or mills. Domestic service was another option for women and girls who might at least be guaranteed a roof over their head. Whatever the job, days were long and money was scarce. This was an era in which healthcare was a privilege, not a right. Thomas Coram's Foundling Hospital was established in 1741 to cope with the number of abandoned babies born to women who couldn't hope to care for them.

Yet advancement was possible, though the gulf from the working class to the middle and even higher was large indeed and precious few climbed the social ranks. For every Dorothy Clement or Gunning sister, where women born into poverty rose to the very top of society thanks to a judicious marriage, there were a thousand unhappy endings.

It was a world in which women had to capitalise on what they had and if that was good looks and chutzpah, it might just be enough. Ambitious men, meanwhile, sought to escape their narrow horizons by joining the army or navy and progressing through the ranks. However, with military commissions on sale to the richest bidder, a man had to distinguish himself to hope to advance this way. Yet it could be done. Just ask Ambrose O'Higgins. Born in County Sligo to a tenant farmer, he ended his days as Viceroy of Chile and, of course, being a man, he didn't have to rely on his good looks to do it.

The teeming streets of Georgian Britain were paved with gold with some and rags for others

Lower class amusements

Fairs
Traditional fairs were an important event in the calendar of working class Georgians. Famed events such as the Bartholomew Fair offered a wealth of entertainment for everyone, from innocent to saucy!

Public executions
Hugely popular public executions were free to view. In London, the condemned were paraded from Newgate to Tyburn through vast crowds and the atmosphere was more carnival than funeral.

Bare knuckle boxing
Ferocious, often ungoverned boxing matches provided unmatched entertainment for Georgians. With both male and female pugilists keen to fight, success in a bout could mean fame and fortune.

CLASS AND ENTERTAINMENT

A day in the life of the lower classes

Go to work

By 6am, workers were beginning their day at the mill, on the farm or wherever they had been lucky enough to gain the employment that would hopefully keep them from total penury. For 13 hours they toiled in backbreaking conditions alongside men, women and children who were subjected to dangerous conditions, powering industries that would help the men at the top claw their way into the upper classes, where money could buy a seat at the richest table.

There was no top table for the lower class worker, of course, and whether in the factory, the mine, the shipyard or the farm, there was noise, heat and danger to contend with, but the rewards were far from generous.

A working day in the 18th century meant long hours of toil for precious little pay

Enjoy a drink at the pub

After a long day at work, who could blame the working class Georgian for relaxing with a strong drink? For those who succumbed to it, gin could be a deceptive mistress. It chased away the cold and filled the empty belly, as well as providing a few hours away from the reality of life in the rookeries and factories. Yet Britain's love of gin led to a rash of alcoholism and with no license required to distil it let alone regulation of production, 18th century gin could be dangerous indeed. The horrors of the gin craze were depicted in Hogarth's nightmarish *Gin Lane* and its cheery sister piece *Beer Street*, which sang the virtues of honest ale over ruinous spirits.

A stark portrayal of the effects of unlicensed gin production among the working class

Watch a boxing match

With overcrowded rooms waiting for them at home, once a working class Georgian had a few gins to warm them, where better to spend the evening than watching fighters or chickens knocking seven bells out of one another? With boxing matches and cockfights alike often held in taverns and alehouses, a patron could sit back with a strong drink, put a meagre bet on the outcome of the bout and dream of a big win. Far from the 21st century, there was an unimaginable hunger for bloodsports in the Georgian era across every class, from the upper class hunting parties on grand estates, to the cockpits in gloomy London lanes, where bloody conflict meant a night of affordable, rowdy entertainment.

Cockfights, bear baiting and even boxing exploited the Georgian public's thirst for blood – whether animal or human!

Take in a show from the galleries

The theatre was a place where all social classes found entertainment, but their experiences couldn't have been more different. As the king sat in the grandest box in Covent Garden, with the upper class patrons alongside, the poor were huddled into the galleries at the highest point in the building. Here they drank, heckled and even occasionally spat onto the upper classes in the boxes below.

Elsewhere, the poor could go to a so-called 'penny theatre', where they paid a penny to enjoy low budget, short productions. If even this was beyond the budget, some taverns hosted their own entertainments, from singers to jugglers and beyond, for patrons to enjoy.

Crammed into the hot, noisy gallery, poorer theatregoers had the most uncomfortable seats in the house

CULTURE & KNOWLEDGE

NO HOLDS BARRED

The blood-splattered truth behind Britain's underground fight club that attracted crowds of thousands – including kings and prime ministers – even after it was outlawed

WRITTEN BY **PAUL EDWARDS** AND **ROBERT LOCK**

On 17 April 1860, boxing's first-ever 'world title' match took place in a field near the small town of Farnborough, Hampshire. Billed as the 'fight of the century', the bout was between all-American champ John Heenan and England's reigning champion Tom Sayers.

The greatest of his generation, at 1.7 metres (5 foot 8 inches) tall and weighing 67 kilograms (147 pounds), Sayers had managed to punch his way up into the heavyweight division. Here he demolished his lumbering opponents through a combination of incredible skill and tenacity. However, that was in the 1850s, and 'Brighton Titch,' as Sayers was nicknamed, was now 33 – old even by modern boxing standards. In contrast, Heenan was in his mid-twenties and at the height of his powers. He was about 1.9 metres (6 feet, 2 inches) and 43 kilograms (195 pounds), with an apparently lethal left hook. Known as the 'Benicia Boy,' Heenan grew up in New York State, but learned to fight in California, where he worked as an 'enforcer' for a San Francisco gang, before taking up the sport. Still, Heenan's training had been sporadic – unlike Sayers – and he didn't have the old pro's experience to fall back on.

The title fight gripped the imagination on both sides of the Atlantic. As Harper's Weekly put it: "The bulk of the people in England and America are heart and soul engrossed in a fight compared to which a Spanish bull-bait is but a mild and diverting pastime." Meanwhile, in Britain, the Manchester Guardian observed that "no pugilistic contest ever decided has excited so great an interest, both in this and other countries."

When the two men were called to the 'scratch' at 7.29am, you couldn't see the green grass of the field for the packed crowd that filled it. The two fighters stood in the middle of a small, roped-off area, stripped down to their waists, but they didn't don gloves - this was a bare-knuckle battle. Both gladiators tore strips out of each other early on: Sayers was forced to fight one-handed when he injured his right arm, while Heenan was half blinded due to a swollen eye. Nonetheless, the pair duked it out for a staggering 42 rounds. Each severely bloodied and battered, they fought tit for tat for two hours and 27 minutes. However, before either champion could land a winning blow, the police arrived, wielding their truncheons, to stop the fight.

Bare-knuckle boxing was illegal, as it had been since it gained popularity in the Georgian Era. However, the fights were regulated by the semi-respectable British Pugilists' Protective Association, reported on in the sport section of newspapers, and drew large crowds, including the great and good. The Heenan vs Sayers clash has been heavily mythologised: various stories claim Parliament shortened its hours so that Prime Minister Lord Palmerston could attend, that novelists Charles Dickens and William Thackeray were both forced to flee the police along with the rest of the audience, while Queen Victoria sat in her palace waiting for news of the result. So how did bare-knuckle boxing come to gain such an allure in the British imagination, and why then did it disappear?

BIRTH OF BOXIANA

The first recorded prize fight in Britain took place in January 1681, with regular matches being staged at the Royal Theatre in London by 1698. However, it is perhaps too generous to call these clashes 'sport'. While we might consider the

A former chapel, known as The Ring in Southwark, London, was a popular Victorian boxing venue

NO HOLDS BARRED

Newspaper sketch of Tom Sayers in his heyday, fighting Tom Paddock in 1858

"Various stories claim Parliament shortened its hours so Lord Palmerston could attend"

Sayers and Heenan bout ultra-violent by modern standards, they at least followed set rules. During and leading up to the 18th century, the only aim was that you had to defeat your opponent – by any means necessary. Wrestling was allowed, so a man could grab and throw his opponent, then jump on and beat him while he was down. Fists were the primary weapon, but fighters would also wield swords, cudgels or quarterstaffs. Outside of the more sophisticated theatres, they would often face each other in an ill-defined ring formed by the crowd, which would be constantly moving as eager fans pressed in or stepped back to avoid being hit. The pair would beat each other to the point where either of them could no longer carry on. The only aspects that we would really recognise – beyond the fighters – was that there was an umpire to adjudicate on who won if both contenders were badly beaten, and that each man had a second, what we would call a cornerman today, who could throw in the towel for their fighter to rescue them while forfeiting the match to the other man.

James Figg was England's greatest champion in this era. Born in Oxfordshire around 1695, probably to a poor farming family, Figg is said to only have lost one fight in a career that encompassed over 270 fights. Figg claimed he only lost because he was ill, and indeed he defeated the victor, Ned Sutton, in a rematch. Figg was even considered famous enough to be painted by William Hogarth on trading cards.

However, Figg got ahead in this anything-goes age because he was technically skilled. The Marquis de Bretagne noted that Figg, "handles a broad sword [sic] with the greatest dexterity of any man alive." By 1714, Figg had moved to London to study with the Company of Masters of the Science of Defence, a guild dating back to Tudor times that trained members to fight proficiently with rapier, quarterstaff and, of course, broadsword. Figg qualified as a 'master' in under a year. While training, Figg also fought at a fair in Southwark. He would lure crowds to his booth by declaring: "Here I am, Jemmy Figg from Thame – I will fight any man in England!"

In 1719, Figg opened an 'academy of arms' just off Oxford Street. Here, he taught pupils – from aspiring professional prize fighters to gentlemen about town – new techniques, adapting what he knew from the art of swordplay for boxing, including how to block and cross-punch.

While Figg raised the quality of the sport, it was one of his students, Jack Broughton, who laid down the rules. Like Figg, he fought at a fairground, but was profoundly affected when he accidentally killed his opponent, George Stephenson, in 1741. When Stephenson – who was another student of Figg's – fell and didn't get up, Broughton is said to have cried, "Good God. What have I done? I've killed him. So help me God, I'll never fight again."

He didn't keep to this oath, but two years later he opened Broughton's Amphitheatre and changed

---

First rules of Fight Club

Jack Broughton's dos and don'ts guided bareknuckle boxing for over a century

✓ DO

Come to scratch
Each boxer had to come to the centre of the ring for the fight to legally continue. If a boxer could not make the scratch under his own efforts, it was quite acceptable for his seconds to drag him there for him to be able to carry on.

The battle begins
No one could be in the ring except the fighter's seconds and the referee. Usually each fighter would have two seconds who stayed in the ring with him at all times, so at each bout there would be, including the fighters, eight or nine people.

It's a knockout
There were disputes as to how long a man should stay on the floor to declare his opponent the winner. From the knockdown, his 'seconds' had 30 seconds to again drag him to his corner and prepare him for the next round.

In the by-battles
The winning fighter should be given two thirds of the money, which would be publicly divided up on stage. This arrangement was acceptable to all parties, but some had side bets that were paid out privately after the fight.

Get it right
Show some humility and understanding in the way in which a boxer wins or loses a fight. It's not always enough to turn a back on an opponent, and in exceptional circumstances the winner may wish to donate some of his purse to the loser.

✗ DON'T

Keep it clean
Once a man is down, it will not be lawful for one man to strike the other. Gouging will not be acceptable, but to grab a fighter by the throat or throw him to the ground is within the rules, though once he is there kicking is prohibited.

Use your feet
Under the Broughton Rules, feet were now strictly for standing on and not used to further injure an opponent, whether he was upright or knocked down. There will be no heavy or spiked objects within the shoe to cause unnecessary harm to the opponent.

Use your head
Head-butting prior to 1743 was an accepted practice, but times were changing, and this manoeuvre was becoming more and more unpopular. Spectators were looking for skill with the fists, not the head. The fight game was progressing in the right direction.

Holding the ropes
Holding the ropes was used to get more momentum from the body when assaulting the opponent. This, coupled with the use of resin on the hands to ensure better grip, was also outlawed and frowned upon from spectators.

Do not bite
Biting was commonplace during fights, and could inflict serious clinical issues to the recipient. This was quite rightly outlawed, as was the use of holding stones in the fists to produce more power in the punch. The fists at the end of a fight would be broken and difficult to open.

89

CULTURE & KNOWLEDGE

boxing forever. The new proprietor outlined seven rules, which he taught to his students and insisted upon being followed in every fight. These still allowed wrestling moves and even hair-pulling, but the weapons were removed and contenders were forbidden to hit a man when he was down or when he was on his knees. Broughton also insisted that a "square of a yard" be chalked in the middle of the stage; when a man was knocked down, he would have half a minute to return to the mark with the help of his second, or be declared defeated. While he only intended to govern bouts taking place in his own ring, the Broughton Rules, as they became known, were quickly adopted by other venues and continued to guide the sport for the next 100 years.

REGENCY ROYAL RUMBLE

In 1750, an Act of Parliament reaffirmed that prize fighting was illegal. The courts would charge contenders with affray or assault, while spectators ran the risk of being classified as disorderly assemblies. The law continued to be widely flouted, but its reiteration may have had something to do with the temporary decline in interest among the gentry. The sport was also beset by corruption at this time, with fight after fight being thrown. Jack Slack, a savage fighter and grandson of James Figg, is credited with being the first known person to fix a fight. He is believed to have paid off better fighters to lose in other matches to stop top contenders challenging his title. After losing it anyway to William Stevens in 1760, Slacks then paid Stevens to take a fall against his protege, George Meggs.

This downturn continued for 30 years until someone came along who could bet on a fight without fear of the law or loss of earnings: the Prince of Wales. The future George IV attended a number of bare-knuckle-boxing matches between 1786 and 1788. Most notably, he watched 'Gentleman' John Jackson's victory over William Futrell on 9 July 1788. With such a prominent figure holding court ringside, 'the Fancy' – as prize fighters called the upper classes – soon came flocking back.

Based on his nickname, it's perhaps unsurprising that the aforementioned 'Gentleman'

> "The Broughton Rules, as they became known, were quickly adoped by venues"

Two men spar on a wintery 26th December - but 'Boxing day' wasn't named for the sport

Daniel Mendoza holds his opponent in a headlock

90

Ben Caunt raises Ben Bendigo up by the neck in an 1845 showdown

Jackson helped legitimise the sport. Originally from a fairly well-to-do family, Jackson ran a boxing academy for gentry, most notably including the infamous poet Lord Byron among his students. For King George IV's coronation, Jackson was asked to assemble guards to keep order, and chose 18 prize fighters.

However, while these fighters won over the nobility, in London's East End, a Jewish fighter of Portuguese descent named Daniel Mendoza pioneered a crucial new technique. Up until this time, boxers had relied on stinging like a bee, not floating like a butterfly. Only 1.7 metres (5 feet 7 inches) tall and weighing 72.5 kilograms (160 pounds), the slight fighter was the first to emphasise rapid, rather than hard, punching, as well as thinking seriously about his footwork so that he could win through speed rather than just brute strength.

With the sport at all-time high, in 1812, journalist Pierce Egan went as far to claim boxing defined British identity. In his book *Boxiana*, Egan wrote that without it the national character might "act too refined and the thorough-bred bulldog degenerate into the whining puppy! Not for the British the long knives of the Dutch, Italian stilettos or French or German sticks and stones – in England the fist only is used [...] As a national trait we feel no hesitation in declaring that it is wholly British!" We can perhaps chalk some of this nationalism up to the fact that Egan was writing during the Napoleonic War, but boxing's hold

TOP 5 PRIZE FIGHTERS
These boxers, without doubt, were the real superstars of their day

TOM CRIBB
8 JULY 1781 – 11 MAY 1848

Born in Bristol to a coal worker father, Tom Cribbs began his career in 1805. It may be debatable whether he would have gained as much prominence if it were not for his two fights against the 'Black American', Tom Molineaux. His defining bout was the Molineaux rematch of 1811 in front of 20,000 fight fans, such was the popularity of the sport. He's still much loved in his home city of Bristol.

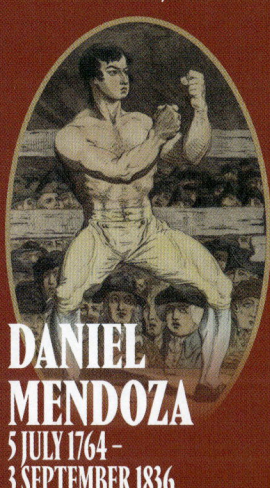

DANIEL MENDOZA
5 JULY 1764 – 3 SEPTEMBER 1836

Dan was the first Jewish champion of England, and possibly the world, depending on how we interpret his fights. He took boxing to another level with his skill, style and speed. He abandoned the wrestling moves and worked on the scientific approach to all his fights. Not the biggest of fighters, he readily took on – and beat – opponents several stone heavier than himself.

TOM MOLINEAUX
1784 – 4 AUGUST, 1818

Molineaux's exact date of birth is unknown, because he was born a slave on a Virginia plantation. However, he became known for fighting other slaves there, and after victory upon victory he was granted his freedom. Two very notable fights against Tom Cribb in 1810 and 1811 at Thistleton Gap in the East Midlands saw 20,000 people witness his defeat of Tom Cribb. He died in Galway in 1818.

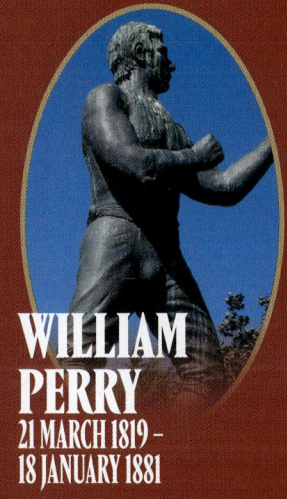

WILLIAM PERRY
21 MARCH 1819 – 18 JANUARY 1881

Known as the 'Tipton Slasher', he became Heavyweight Champion of England in 1850 after beating Tom Paddock. Soon after this, he suffered a controversial defeat to Henry Broome on a referee's decision. Later he regained the coveted title, before eventually losing it to Tom Sayers in 1857. He was born with a severe deformity in his left leg that impacted his walk, which led some people to refer to him as 'K Legs'.

JOHN GULLY
21 AUGUST 1783 – 9 MARCH 1863

Another Bristolian, in his early years he was imprisoned in a debtor's institution, but later became a prize fighter. The Duke of Clarence (later King William IV) witnessed his brutal 64-round fight against Henry Pearce in 1805. In the latter half of his life, he was an entrepreneur and race horse owner. He also became a politician, and sat in the House of Commons as the MP for Pontefract from 1832 to 1837.

CULTURE & KNOWLEDGE

upon the British imagination is evidenced in the many idioms taken from the sport that entered the English language during this period. Phrases such as 'start from scratch' (to start over from the beginning), and 'not up to the mark' (not up to the necessary level) may refer to the line that was scratched in the dirt to divide the ring. It's said the term 'draw', meaning a tied score, derives from the stakes that held the rope surrounding the ring; when the match was over, the stakes were 'drawn' out from the ground. These stakes might also be the basis behind the monetary meaning of stakes. In early prize fights, a bag of money, which would go to the winner of the bout, was hung from one of the stakes – thus high stakes and stake money.

The Regency era (1811-20) proved to be a golden age for bare-knuckle boxing, producing a constellation of superstars, including Tom Belcher, Tom Cribb, John Gully, and Bill Richmond – another former slave who spent most of his career in Britain. However, it was the year of Queen Victoria's coronation, 1838, that saw bare-knuckle boxing take a step forward. The London Prize Ring rules – also called the London Rules for brevity – were quickly adopted on both sides of the Atlantic, introducing a larger 7.3-metre (24-foot) ring enclosed by rope, declaring that fallen fighters should be able to return to the mark unaided or forfeit the match, and forbid butting, gouging, hitting below the waist and kicking as fouls.

KO IN THE UK

After the police interrupted Sayers and Heenan's fight for the world title in 1860, there was a dispute over who actually won. Officially, the referee declared it a draw, but Heenan demanded a rematch. This never happened, instead the pair both received a championship belt and split the 'purse' of £400 – over £20,000 in today's money. When Heenan returned to the United States he was given a hero's welcome anyway and 50,000 New Yorkers came out to welcome him.

Bare-knuckle boxing was a fixture of British sport for 200 years

Meanwhile, Sayers fans raised £3,000 so that the veteran fighter could retire. However, the next five years did not go so well for him. Sayers was estranged from his wife and had several other acrimonious break-ups, suffered from diabetes and tuberculosis, made a failed investment in a circus, and developed a drinking problem. He died living above a shop on Camden High Street at the age of 39, with his two children and his father by his side. What was left of Sayers' still sizeable fortune was spent on an extravagant funeral. Some 100,000 people took part in his procession

Female boxing was not often taken seriously

Birth of Women's Boxing

Very little is known about women's boxing during the 19th century, perhaps because it was seen as a sideshow and not reflective of the way men went about their fights. Some of these tough women fought bare chested and, by some illogical reasoning, wore long dresses down to the floor to hide their modesty. Many prostitutes also took part in the matches. Usually the women would fight with a coin in each hand, and the first to drop it would be deemed the loser.

The first recorded fight between two females took place in 1722 near what is now, Oxford Circus between Elizabeth Wilkinson and Martha Jones. Wilkinson won the contest and was considered to be the first female champion, and she fought fully clothed, so the audience would take her more seriously. Wilkinson would have been born around 1700, but the details of her birth cannot be proved with any certainty. However, it seems she became a very formidable fighter not only with her fists, but also with a dagger, cudgel and quarterstaff. Elizabeth went on to marry a pugilist named Stokes, who fought in James Figg's boxing booth and eventually set up her own booth to rival Figg's.

In 1722 she handed out a challenge to Hannah Hyfield of Newgate Market. It was usual for women's fights to last between 20 minutes and an hour, and Elizabeth's strength and fitness far exceeded the low expectations of female stamina at the time. Elizabeth Wilkinson Stokes, as she became known, had a close rival in Mary Welsh (who, ironically, was Irish). The two women fought, along with their husbands, forming 'mixed-doubled' pairs. From all accounts it seems Welsh won the battle, although this cannot be proven with any certainty.

The illegal sport attracted high society fans in the 18th Century

NO HOLDS BARRED

Padded gloves were introduced as a safety measure under the 1867 Queensberry Rules

Jake Kilrain takes on John Sullivan in 1889, the last recognised bareknuckle fight

as Sayer's loyal mastiff dog, Lion, wearing a crepe ruff, led his coffin to Highgate Cemetery.

In some ways, the fates of the two men signalled the shift in bare-knuckle boxing's fortunes in the two countries. Corruption once again emerged in the British sport, with more fights being rigged. Meanwhile, Victorian moralists decried bare-knuckle boxing for its violence. Seizing on growing popular opinion, Parliament increasingly penalised the game in such a way that every fight fan or fighter would be arrested and dealt with accordingly if caught in the act of promoting or supporting a prize fight.

After Sayer, Britain still produced a few acclaimed bruisers, most notably Tom King and Jem Mace. Facing growing persecution at home and the promise of greater cash prizes abroad, these fighters increasingly went to the US. The sport was illegal there too, but the law varied state by state, and in some places it was quite lax. Mace courted the fame the sport brought in the US, where he continued to fight until he was well into his 60s.

In 1882, rising Boston talent John L Sullivan beat Irish-born Paddy Ryan in a highly publicised bout in Mississippi City. The New York Times claimed some $300,000 was wagered across America on the fight, while telegraph circuits surged to deliver blow-by-blow accounts to eager fans that filled the streets. At last, it seemed America had embraced prize fighting and the spiritual home of the sport had finally moved across the Atlantic. However, at this point the sport's days were numbered all around the world.

"In some way, the fates of two men signalled the shift in bare-knuckle boxing's fortunes"

In 1867, the Marquess of Queensberry endorsed a new set of rules for boxing. Though actually written by a Welsh sportsman named John Graham Chambers, the most important detail of the Queensberry Rules was the biggest change to the sport since Jack Broughton laid down the law in 1743. It demanded that all fighters wear padded boxing gloves.

While bare-knuckle fighting didn't end overnight, Jem Mace was quick to see that the writing was on the wall. Changing his tactics, the former English heavyweight champion defeated the formidable Bill Davis in Virginia City, Nevada, under the Queensberry Rules in 1876. The last bare-knuckle fight took place on British soil in 1885 between champion Jem Smith and Jack Davis. Smith won easily, but few were there to witness the spectacle.

The Queensberry code came into force in the United States and Canada in the late 19th century, with the last recognised bare-knuckle encounter taking place on 8 July 1889, between Jake Kilrain and John L Sullivan. Fought using the London Rules, this contest ran until an incredible 76 rounds, when Kilrain's second threw in the sponge, saying his man would die if the bout went on any longer. With that, bare-knuckle boxing was served its final KO.

Or was it? That was the case until June 2018, when the first legal bare-knuckle boxing match was held in the US - almost 130 years since the last match. Arnold Adams and DJ Lindermann met for their showdown in the prairie city of Cheyenne, Wyoming. 2,000 fans crammed into the converted ice rink, and after a gruelling set, Arnold Adams won. Other states in the US are now looking to legalise the fights.

With bare-knuckle boxing poised to get back in the fighting ring once again, it is all the more important to recall the working-class origins of the bloody sport.

The East End slums where many British bare-knuckle fighters grew up

CULTURE & KNOWLEDGE

Austen's novels remain some of the most popular in the world, two centuries after her death

Defining moments

A stumbling block, 1803
Austen's brother, Henry, sold the copyright to her novel *Susan* to publisher Crosby & Sons for £10, with the promise of an early publication. However, Crosby did not publish the book at all and Austen lacked the means to buy the copyright back from him. *Susan* remained in Crosby's possession until 1816, when Henry managed to buy the copyright back after the publication of *Emma*.

The first publication, 1811
Austen self-funded the publication of her first novel, *Sense and Sensibility*, and paid the publisher Thomas Egerton a commission on the sales. Novels were usually published with 500 editions, but *Sense and Sensibility* was published with 750, all of them had sold by July 1813. Austen gained a taste of financial independence with a profit of £140.

A literary success, 1814
After the successful publication of *Pride and Prejudice* in January 1813, Thomas Egerton agreed to publish Austen's next novel, *Mansfield Park*, the first novel she had written as an adult at Chawton. *Mansfield Park*'s first run sold out within six months and it earned Austen more money than any of her other novels, though reviewers ignored it until 1821.

JANE AUSTEN

Uncovering the life and work of the iconic author whose novels changed the literary world

WRITTEN BY **JESSICA LEGGETT**

The works of Jane Austen have kept generations of people around the world entertained with the unique blend of witty humour, irony and social realism that defined her writing. It was during Austen's lifetime that novels began to take off as a major form of entertainment and in the two centuries since her death, she has without a doubt become one of Britain's best loved novelists.

It is impossible to discuss Austen's work without looking at her life, which influenced much of her writing. She was born on 16 December 1775 in the village of Steventon in Hampshire, to George and Cassandra Austen, the seventh of eight children. Her father was a clergyman who made a modest living, so to provide extra income, the family residence also doubled as a small school for boys.

When Austen was around eight years old, her beloved older sister Cassandra was sent to Oxford for her education. Refusing to part with her, Austen went too and the pair almost died when they caught typhus. After this, the girls home educated until they left for boarding school in 1785, returning on account of the school's expensive fees.

Austen developed a passion for reading from an early age, encouraged by her father and older brothers. She enjoyed writing stories and poems and would read them aloud to her family. Among one of her first works was her short epistolary novel, *Lady Susan*, which she wrote between 1793 and 1795. Afterwards, Austen began writing her very first novel, *Elinor and Marianne*.

It was around this time, in December 1795, that Austen was introduced to Tom Lefroy, a student who was heading to London to train as a barrister. Lefroy made several visits to Steventon over the next month and there was a clear attraction between the two. Their relationship was eventually cut short when his family intervened and sent Lefroy away – a match between the two was not ideal, particularly as neither of them had any money, and Austen never saw him again.

Austen had finished her revisions for *Elinor and Marianne* and completed the drafts for her novels *First Impressions* and *Susan*, a satire for the popular gothic novel, by 1799. When her father announced his retirement the following year, Austen moved with her sister and parents to Bath, although she was upset to leave the only home she had ever known.

Two years later, Austen accepted a proposal from her childhood friend, Harris Bigg-Wither, even though she had no romantic feelings for him. Bigg-Wither was in line for a sizeable inheritance and this appealed to Austen, who wanted to secure her family's future. However, Austen revoked her acceptance the next day after sleeping on her decision. This is the only known proposal Austen received and she remained single for the rest of her life, aside from a reported romance with a stranger during her time in Bath.

Austen was unproductive in Bath compared to her time in Steventon and she barely wrote anything save for a brief attempt at a novel, *The*

The cottage in Chawton where Austen lived for the last eight years of her life, and is now a museum in her honour

Watsons, which was left unfinished. It has been claimed that Austen's ability to write was affected because she was unhappy in Bath, or because she was simply too busy to focus on her work, however we do not know the reason for certain.

After her father's sudden death in 1805, Austen moved frequently with her mother and sister before settling in a cottage located on her brother Edward's estate in Chawton, in 1809. While living here, Jane oversaw the successful publications of *Elinor and Marianne* and *First Impressions*, which were retitled as *Sense and Sensibility* and *Pride and Prejudice*, as well as her new novels *Mansfield Park* and *Emma*, in 1811, 1813, 1814 and 1815 respectively. All were published anonymously, with the title page of *Sense and Sensibility* simply stating that it was written 'By a Lady'.

At the beginning of 1816, Austen noticed that she was unwell but chose to ignore her symptoms, persevering with her next novel, *The Elliots*. She completed the first draft that July and over the next two months she rewrote the final two chapters. By January 1817, Austen had picked up her pen and paper again, starting on a new novel titled *The Brothers*.

Sadly, Austen's health seriously declined and she was forced to stop writing *The Brothers* after completing 12 chapters. Lacking energy and struggling to walk, Austen was confined to her bed by April and the next month, she was moved to Winchester by Cassandra and her brother Henry to seek treatment. This proved to be futile, as Austen succumbed to her illness on 18 July 1817, aged just 41. Exactly what she suffered from is undetermined, but it is believed that Austen may have had Addison's disease.

Henry arranged for his sister to be buried in Winchester Cathedral and with Cassandra, they set about organising the publication of Austen's remaining completed novels, *Susan* and *The Elliots*. Published together in 1818, they were renamed *Northanger Abbey* and *Persuasion*, accompanied with a biographical note written by Henry, identifying Austen as the author of all six novels for the first time.

Austen's life had a huge impact on her writing style and although she was known for her love of satire, it was her distinctive use of social realism that won her acclaim from contemporary critics. Her ability to incorporate ordinary life into her novels entranced her readers, who imagined themselves experiencing the same conversations and events as the characters. This is why Austen's novels are set in the south of England, with both *Northanger Abbey* and *Persuasion* set in Bath, because this is where she had lived and could therefore accurately write about life there.

In addition, some of Austen's fictional characters are believed to have been based on people in her life. For example, the sisters Elinor and Marianne Dashwood in *Sense and Sensibility* are often compared to Cassandra and Austen herself, with Marianne's romance with Mr Willoughby commonly seen as a reflection of her fleeting relationship with Tom Lefroy.

Furthermore, two of Austen's brothers, Francis and Charles, were in the Royal Navy during the Napoleonic Wars, which may have influenced

Special gift editions of Austen's novels were published in the Victorian era - this illustration is from the 1896 edition of Emma

JANE AUSTEN

Austen moved to Bath with her parents and sister at the turn of the 19th century

Austen's burnt letters

One of the surviving letters from Jane to her beloved sister Cassandra, dated 11 June 1799

her decision to make many of her characters officers. For example, Mr Wickham, from *Pride and Prejudice*, is a militia officer and Captain Wentworth, from *Persuasion*, makes his fortune as a naval officer during the wars.

Nonetheless, it is incorrect to deem Austen a realist writer since all of her novels had an idealistic ending. Her heroines always married for love rather than for social status or money, perhaps indicating that Austen herself believed in the importance of affection. This is possibly suggested by her own broken engagement – even though her female contemporaries were faced with the reality of status and financial security when it came to marriage.

Among Austen's admirers was the Prince Regent, who kept a set of her novels at every one of his residences. In 1815 his librarian, James Stanier Clarke, invited Austen to dedicate her forthcoming novel *Emma* to the prince. As she could not turn it down, Austen begrudgingly wrote the dedication even though she disliked the prince for his treatment of his estranged wife, Princess Caroline.

However, not everyone was completely taken with Austen's novels. Fellow author and literary legend Charlotte Brontë read *Pride and Prejudice* upon the recommendation of critic GH Lewes and was left very disappointed. An unimpressed Brontë did not hold back with her opinion of the novel and said to Lewes; "I should hardly like to live with her ladies and gentlemen in their elegant but confined houses."

Brontë was always frustrated whenever her novel, *Jane Eyre*, was compared to Austen. Others have also voiced their criticism over Austen's novels, including writers DH Lawrence and Virginia Woolf. These critics believed that Austen's writing was restricted to the small, elite world of her characters. Though her novels were centred around the elite, money and the necessity of marriage for young women, it was because this was her reality.

Considering the debate around her work that has continued to this day, it might be surprising to learn that Austen was not considered a great novelist during her lifetime, although her books sold fairly well. Her tombstone in Winchester Cathedral does not even mention her career as an author, perhaps because her family did not deem it important enough, or even because that's not how they wanted her to be remembered.

This all changed after Austen's nephew, James Edward Austen-Leigh, published a biography on his aunt in 1869. Brought to the attention of the Victorians, Austen's novels were subsequently reissued and they flew off the shelves, finally achieving the fame they deserved. Three years after the biography was released, a memorial tablet was placed on the wall next to Austen's grave, which finally shone a light on Jane Austen, the author.

> "Austen was not considered a great novelist during her lifetime"

The memorial plaque dedicated to Austen at Winchester Cathedral

With little available sources to refer to, there are unfortunately large gaps in Austen's life that cannot be accounted for. One of the best resources we have to provide an insight into her world and everyday life is her letters, which exist thanks to her prolific correspondence with her sister, Cassandra.

However, we only have around 160 of them because Cassandra destroyed the rest of the letters after Austen's death, as well as her own responses, and edited the remaining ones. It is impossible to determine what drove Cassandra to do such a thing, with most guesses focusing on the idea that she may have been protecting her sister's reputation, if the letters contained sensitive or revealing material.

As Austen's surviving letters showcase her wit and irony, many have mourned the loss of her other letters and have subsequently criticised Cassandra for her actions. However, it has to be remembered that Cassandra also preserved a lot of her sister's work, helping her brother to publish Austen's final two novels posthumously.

It is Cassandra we have to thank for assuming more of the household duties and therefore enabling her sister to devote more of her time to writing. We may question Cassandra's actions but she did it out of love – in a letter written after Austen's death, she sadly noted that her sister "was the sun of my life, the gilder of ever pleasure, the soother of every sorrow."

CULTURE & KNOWLEDGE

THE YEAR WITHOUT SUMMER

As the sky turned black and rain lashed at the shutters, four exiles began telling spooky stories – a competition that birthed one of the undisputed masterpieces of English literature: Frankenstein

WRITTEN BY JAMES HOARE

One summer night in 1816 lighting arced across the surface of Lake Geneva as a monster was born.

High above the lake, a band of misfits gathered around the fireplace in the elegant Villa Diodati, the home of the infamous rake, philanderer and poet Lord Byron. The party had spent endless days and nights cooped up together, besieged by the unusually dismal summer.

In all likelihood they were unaware of the causes, the eruption of Mount Tambora in Indonesia in 1815 had filled the upper atmosphere with volcanic ash, stifling the sun. The rain was torrential, the light dim and harvests failed. It was portentous, like the *Book of Revelations* was unspooling around them.

Byron's poem *Darkness*, written in July 1816, captured a growing sense of unease as, "Morn came and went - and came, and brought no day. And men forgot their passions in the dread. Of this their desolation…"

Lord Byron held court alongside his physician, Dr John Polidori, and his fellow poet, the intense and brooding Percy Bysshe Shelley. Shelley was accompanied by his teenage paramour, Mary Godwin - the two had fled England, leaving behind Shelley's wife - and her step-sister, Claire Clairmont, who harboured ambitions to be the latest of Byron syphilitic conquests.

The 18-year-old Mary Godwin could more than hold her own. Her mother, Mary Wollstonecraft, was an early feminist, and her father, William Godwin, a prominent liberal philosopher. Godwin educated her himself, noting approvingly that she was "singularly bold, somewhat imperious, and active of mind. Her desire of knowledge is great, and her perseverance in everything she undertakes almost invincible".

Shelley, as with many of the great poets and philosophers of the day, was a regular visitor to the Godwin home and the two fell in love. According to popular legend, the then 17-year-old lost her virginity to the penniless 22-year-old radical on the grave of her mother. Godwin disapproved - among other things, Shelley had promised and failed to pay off his immense debts - and the two eloped, taking Mary's step-sister with them, leaving Shelley's pregnant wife.

Described by Mary as possessing "wild, intellectual, unearthly looks", the reality of life with Percy soon bit. She was pregnant, Shelley was clearly sleeping with her step-sister, his wife, Harriet, had given birth, and he was trying to set her up with one of their mutual friends who she initially despised. She believed in free love in principle, but in reality Percy was her soulmate and she had to swallow down the pain in the name of love.

Their child was born two months premature and soon died, plunging Mary into deep depression. With an echo of the themes that would later make her famous, she wrote in her diary: "[I had a] dream that my little baby came to life again; that it had only been cold, and that we rubbed it before the fire, and it lived."

By the summer of 1816 and the party on the shores of Lake Geneva, she had recovered - as much as anyone can recover from such a trauma - but at 18 she had lived, loved and endured much.

The dim half-light of the so-called 'Year Without Summer' must have fit her mood perfectly. The long and gloomy evening became increasingly intense. Polidori had grown infatuated with Mary, Clairmont remained obsessed with Byron, and Shelley slipped ever further into the grip of anxiety as the environment seemed to press down on his fragile mind.

The mood leant itself to morbidity and the assembled poured over *Fantasmagoriana* (1812), a French anthology of German ghost stories. One evening Byron treated them to a theatrical reading of Samuel Taylor Coleridge's poem *Christabel*, in which a predatory serpent of Greek mythology - the Lamia - seeks to possess the innocent Christabel. Lost in the moment, Shelley fled the room screaming, claiming later that he had become transfixed by the image of a woman with eyes where her nipples should have been.

Byron issued the group with a challenge to go off and write a ghost story - pestering them each morning for their progress. Mary gave it so much more than either of the great poets gathered among them - and the good doctor acquitted himself pretty well too.

Byron produced a fragmentary vampire story (published, unfinished, in a 1819 collection) inspired by a folk tale he had heard when travelling in the Balkans, while Polidori offered *The Vampyre* (published 1819), in which a thinly disguised parody of Byron, Lord Ruthven, arrives in London to prey on society ladies. Polidori's effort is regarded the first literary vampire story, creating tone and tropes that would inspire Bram Stoker in the writing of *Dracula*.

CULTURE & KNOWLEDGE

Did Percy Shelley write Frankenstein?

For as long as women have stuck their heads above the parapet, people have been all too eager to credit their achievements to men.

Frankenstein was initially published anonymously in 1818 and when one critic suggested that Percy Shelley was the author, Mary snapped back in a letter that, "I am anxious to prevent your continuing in the mistake of supposing Mr Shelley guilty of a juvenile attempt of mine; to which – from its being written at an early age – I abstained from putting my name."

There's no denying that Percy played an important role in *Frankenstein*, and his notes and edits can be seen on the original manuscript, but there's no real reason to suspect it was written by anyone other than Mary. The notes and letters between the two represent an active dialogue between writer and editor, with Mary assuring her husband, "I give you carte blanche to make what alterations you please". None of which makes the slightest bit of sense if Percy were the real author.

Those who argue that the book's strident tones on liberty and the creator's responsibility to its creation are proof of Percy Shelley's hand, seem to ignore that the two were clearly of similar mind – and that both clearly owe a great debt to her father, the political philosopher William Godwin.

Reginald Easton's 1857 miniature of Mary Shelley is allegedly drawn from her death mask

Page of the original manuscript of Frankenstein: Or, The Modern Prometheus

Italian scientist Luigi Galvani used electrodes to stimulate the muscles of a dead frog, causing the legs to twitch

Mary, however, wrote what would become *Frankenstein: Or, The Modern Prometheus* (published 1818), a potent culmination of ideas, fears and personal tragedy.

"Night waned upon this talk," she explained in the 1831 preface to the novel, "and even the witching hour had gone by before we retired to rest. When I placed my head on my pillow I did not sleep, nor could I be said to think. My imagination, unbidden, possessed and guided me, gifting the successive images that arose in my mind with a vividness far beyond the usual bounds of reverie. I saw – with shut eyes, but acute mental vision – I saw the pale student of the unhallowed arts kneeling beside the thing he had put together. I saw the hideous phantasm of a man stretched out, and then, on the working of some powerful engine show signs of life and stir with an uneasy, half-vital motion." Shelley didn't write anything, but he did encourage Mary to expand her short story into a full novel.

Over the unnaturally cold June nights during their stay at Villa Diodati, the group discussed philosophy, science and emerging pseudosciences,

> *"They discussed philosophy, science and emerging pseudosciences"*

with Dr Polidori acting as a foil to the outlandish pronouncements of Byron and Shelley. The humanist ideals of the American and French Revolutions had stolen authority from kings and gifted them to the common man, and the emerging fields of scientific study conspired to seize authority from God himself.

In 1780, Luigi Galvani conducted one of the first experiments into bioelectricity when he used an electric shock to stimulate the muscles of a dead frog, making them jerk and twitch as if returned to life. Later, in 1803, Giovanni Aldini performed a far more gruesome feat with the corpse of a hanged man, making him lift a leg, an arm and open one eye in a parody of life. To many, it seemed like electricity might really hold the key to reanimation of the dead.

Beyond galvanism, the Scottish surgeon Dr John Hunter had pioneered transplants – creating a boom industry in the wealthy buying healthy teeth from the poor to replace their own rotten chompers – and artificial insemination.

Much of *Frankenstein* reflects the summer by Lake Geneva – it is after all the home of Victor Frankenstein, and many of the Swiss locations described in the novel were visited by Mary. The long and energetic debates about reanimation and pseudoscience, by the flash of the electrical storms, underwrote the central premise of the text. The character of Victor Frankenstein straddles the high ideals of the Enlightenment and the lusts of the Romantic period, inspired by Percy. Shelley first published his work under

THE YEAR WITHOUT SUMMER

the pen name Victor, and like Frankenstein he had a beloved sister called Elizabeth. Both men were born to noble families who grew to scorn them, and while at Eton Shelley conducted experiments in electricity and explosives. It's not an entirely flattering portrait; it is, after all, Frankenstein's hubris and obsession that unleashes a tidal wave of misery.

That however is what makes *Frankenstein* truly remarkable as a novel. As much as it is a masterpiece of Gothic horror, romantic fiction, or science fiction, it also truly captures the voice and pain of this incredible young woman.

A satirical cartoon from 1836 warns of the danger of corpses reanimated by galvanism

Mary Shelley at the age of 42 by painter Richard Rothwell

The holidaymakers of Villa Diodati

LORD BYRON
Famously described as 'mad, bad and dangerous to know', George Gordon Byron was infamous not just for his incredible body of work, but for his several scandalous sexual liaisons with men and women alike, including having a child with his half-sister. By 21, he had both gonorrhoea and syphilis, but it did little to dim his charisma or celebrity.

PERCY BYSSHE SHELLEY
Shelley was a political radical from aristocratic stock who caused scandal by embracing free love and abandoning his wife and children to gallivant around Europe with Mary and Claire. One of the greatest Romantic poets, the heart-rending beauty of his work is compounded by his tragic death by drowning at the age of 29.

JOHN WILLIAM POLIDORI
Byron's personal physician and travelling companion, Polidori kept a diary of his European travels for publication, but it was heavily censored and the original was lost. His entry to the 'ghost story' challenge, *The Vampyre*, is one of the most influential vampire novels of all time, although it was originally attributed to Byron.

CLAIRE CLAIRMONT
Daughter of William Godwin's second wife Mary, Clairmont had an affair with Byron in Britain and urged her step-sister to take her to Switzerland so she could have a shot at becoming his mistress. She had a daughter by Byron in 1817, but he refused to see her and only accepted Allegra on the condition that Clairmont keep her distance.

101

CULTURE & KNOWLEDGE

Literary Icons

During the Regency era, some of Britain's greatest writers produced their most significant works... and changed the face of literature while they were at it

WRITTEN BY **MARK DOLAN**

It's a good thing that reading was a popular pastime in the Regency period, because it was awash with some of the greatest writers in the English language. It was also a time of great innovation and change in literature. While the Romantic poets were gallivanting around Europe, penning odes and telling each other ghost stories, women up and down the country were writing scathing satires of upper-class life, and Gothic tales of mystery and horror were keeping candles burning all night. In this article, we'll take a short tour of some of the most popular, influential and creative writers of this fascinating era.

ANN RADCLIFFE
1764-1823

One of the writers who had the greatest impact on Regency-era literature did not, ironically, publish a book in the Regency period. Ann Radcliffe was one of the most popular authors of the day, her books were bestsellers and she was regarded by the likes of John Keats as one of the most influential writers of their time. Such was her popularity that in 1794, at just 30, she negotiated a fee of £500 with her publishers for her masterpiece, *The Mysteries of Udolpho*. According to the Bank of England's inflation calculator, this would be around £56,000 today, and it was twice the sum that Jane Austen would receive for *Pride and Prejudice* 20 years later.

In fact, Austen was a fan – her love for Radcliffe's work is evident in *Northanger Abbey*, where *Udolpho* features heavily and even directly inspires the Gothic tone of Austen's early (though joint-last published) novel. Gothic novels are the genre with which Radcliffe is most associated, but she did not simply write in an established genre. She took the Gothic elements of Horace Walpole (often regarded as the originator of the style) and combined them with elements of romance, suspense and the supernatural, creating a new, innovative genre.

A suitably dramatic engraving from an 1806 edition of *The Mysteries of Udolpho*

LITERARY ICONS

FANNY BURNEY
1752-1840

Such was Frances 'Fanny' Burney's renown and status, that by 1885 she was a recipient of a blue plaque (though hers is actually red). Burney wrote prolifically throughout her youth, but embarrassed by her unladylike activities, she wrote in secret, scared that her father would discover her hobby. In 1778, she anonymously published her first book, *Evelina*, a satirical novel about the marriage market and the foibles of the upper class. The book quickly found fame, fortune and literary renown. The eminent painter, Joshua Reynolds, couldn't put it down, and Dr Johnson thought it beyond the work of Henry Fielding or Samuel Richardson. *Evelina* was such a success, that Burney became a sensation, and was adored throughout Britain's literary society.

She followed *Evelina* with *Cecilia* in 1782, which confirmed her talent, and grew both her reputation and her profits. One of her young readers was Jane Austen, who took the title of *Pride and Prejudice* from the final pages of *Cecilia*. Burney's influence on the development of British literature, particularly on Austen, led Virginia Woolf to describe her as "the mother of English fiction". Burney wrote one final novel, *The Wanderer*, which appeared in 1814, the same year as *Mansfield Park*.

Fanny Burney, painted by her cousin, c.1784

An engraving of Maria Edgeworth

MARIA EDGEWORTH
1768-1849

Maria Edgeworth was an Anglo-Irish woman who spent her life between the two countries. Born in Oxfordshire, her family settled in Ireland during her adolescence. She was close with her father, the writer and politician Richard Lovell Edgeworth, and the two worked closely together, producing an influential treatise on education, 'Practical Education', in 1798. She soon began writing fiction, for children and adults, at an astonishing rate.

A writer firmly ensconced in the literary intelligentsia of the period, she conversed with Jane Austen and Fanny Burney, who admired her, and directly influenced Sir Walter Scott, whose novel *Waverley* (1814) - one of the earliest historical novels and a major landmark in English literature - was modelled on Edgeworth's *The Absentee* (1812). Her trademark style, which dealt with moral questions and placed an emphasis on the educational potential of fiction, had a significant influence on the development of realism, which went on to grow in popularity throughout the 19th century.

CULTURE & KNOWLEDGE

WILLIAM WORDSWORTH
1770-1850

In 1798, William Wordsworth, alongside his friend and collaborator Samuel Taylor Coleridge, revolutionised English literature when their joint book, *Lyrical Ballads*, began the Romantic movement. Wordsworth contributed the majority of the poems, and the style, subject matter and vocabulary used in the book set a new path for English poetry; one that would inspire the next generation of Romantics, including John Keats, Lord Byron and Percy Bysshe Shelley.

Wordsworth's magnum opus is his long poem, 'The Prelude', an autobiographical poem that he worked on for over 40 years. The title given to the poem was his wife's, and was added after his death. During his lifetime, Wordsworth referred to the piece as simply the 'Poem to Coleridge'.

Unlike some of the later Romantic poets, Wordsworth was lucky to live long enough to be highly regarded in his lifetime, and in 1843 he was named Poet Laureate by then-prime minister, Robert Peel. He initially declined the honour on the grounds of being too old, but Peel informed him it was Queen Victoria's express desire that he take the title and that nothing would be required of him. He therefore accepted and remained Laureate until his death seven years later, without having written any new verse.

A young William Wordsworth

SUSAN EDMONSTONE FERRIER
1782-1854

Susan Edmonstone Ferrier is no longer a household name, but she was one of the most popular novelists of the Regency period, and has been dubbed Scotland's Jane Austen. Ferrier did not have the drive to be a literary great that some of her contemporaries had, and she only wrote her first novel, *Marriage* (1818) after a friend, Charlotte Clavering, suggested they co-write a novel. Ferrier did not enjoy the process, and completed the novel herself. When it was published in Edinburgh, anonymously, in 1818, it was an immediate hit. The run of 1,500 copies sold out in six months, and readers attempted to guess the author's identity. Many ascribed it to Walter Scott, Scotland's premier novelist at the time, and a friend of Ferrier's father. Scott was in fact a great fan of Ferrier's writing, and an avid supporter of her work.

Marriage was a very satirical, sardonic novel, and Ferrier's second and third books, *Inheritance* (1824) and *Destiny* (1831), followed suit. They were also well received, and are still highly regarded - if not that popular - to this day.

Susan Ferrier, 'Scotland's Jane Austen'

LITERARY ICONS

JOHN KEATS
1795-1821

Few people have made as large an impact in just 25 years of life as John Keats. Having initially trained as a physician, Keats was set instead on the artistic life, and had the depressive episodes and sensitive nature that went with the territory. Now considered a key part of the second generation of the Romantic movement, along with Byron and Shelley, and following in the footsteps of Coleridge and Wordsworth, Keats had just 54 poems published in his lifetime. However, in that time he took on a range of styles and developed so quickly and remarkably that his lyricism is now held up alongside that of Shakespeare.

Keats's fortunes during his lifetime were poor. At the time of his death, it's estimated that the combined sales of his three books were around 200 – but his legacy grew quickly.

His odes, for which he's best known, including 'On Indolence', 'On a Grecian Urn' and 'To a Nightingale', and his best long poems, 'Lamia' and 'Hyperion', were all written in 1819 during the time he met and fell in love with his muse, Fanny Brawne. It was around the same time, however, that his health began to sharply decline. He wrote no more after 1819 and finally succumbed to tuberculosis in early 1821.

An oil painting of John Keats

LORD BYRON
1788-1824

Lord Byron ranks among the greatest, most recognisable and fascinatingly complex writers Britain has ever produced. Born into the aristocracy, he was educated the accepted way, making his way through Harrow and then Cambridge University. It was here that Byron carried out one of his most unique acts of defiance, one that had no bearing on his poetry but that says a lot about the man. Upon being informed that he couldn't bring his beloved dog to his college, Byron proceeded to purchase a bear instead, which wasn't explicitly banned. When his college asked what to do with his new friend, Byron responded that "he should sit for a fellowship".

Byron wrote prolifically throughout his life, developing his talent and producing some of the most popular poetry of the era. His creative output hit its apex in 1819, with the publication of the first two volumes of 'Don Juan', a long satirical poem about the fictional Spanish lothario, Don Juan. The poem is Byron's masterpiece, and is one of the most renowned epic poems of all time. He was part of the Romantic movement, alongside poets such as Coleridge, Shelley and Keats, and his literary circle added as much to his legacy as did his poetry. He was part of the story of Mary Shelley coming up with the idea for *Frankenstein*, and became one of the first true celebrities through his combination of talent, eccentricity and penchant for scandal. His wife, Annabella, described the public interest as 'Byromania', while one of his lovers, Lady Caroline Lamb, famously described him as "mad, bad and dangerous to know".

Lord Byron, c. 1813

CULTURE & KNOWLEDGE

Constable turned his back on a lucrative career in portraiture to follow his love of landscapes

REGENCY ARTISTS

During the Regency era, Romanticism was at its height; the movement made superstars of some artists

WRITTEN BY **CATHERINE CURZON**

In the Regency era, wealth and status were held in high regard and while it didn't do to be too ostentatious - unless you were the Prince Regent - subtly showing off what you were worth by displaying paintings by the most celebrated artists of the day was one way to ensure everyone knew you were somebody. *Bridgerton* fans have revelled in the character portraits that can be seen hanging on the walls of the grand houses, perfectly recreating the style of the likes of Sir Thomas Lawrence; in the Regency Period, Romanticism had arrived.

In the years before the Regency era, art and architecture had turned towards Neoclassicism, celebrating the straight, clean lines and geometric shapes and styles of the ancient world. By the end of the 18th century, however, celebration of the classical had started to change and tastemakers

REGENCY ARTISTS

wanted something different. They turned to Romanticism, which rejected the mathematically governed, geometrically perfect lines of Neoclassicism. Emerging partly as a reaction to the stark reality of the Industrial Revolution, the Romantic movement harked back to a different time altogether and encouraged its followers to think for themselves, rather than blindly following the prevailing trend. Followers of the movement valued their individualism and firmly believed that it should be expressed at every opportunity.

The Romantics longed for the Middle Ages and an era of chivalry and courtliness. They rejected the rationalism of the Age of Enlightenment but instead encouraged people to look backwards, rather than forwards, and recapture what had been lost. They championed artists and authors as heroes and true cultural leaders, bringing them to the forefront of the movement and into the orbit of the chattering classes.

When it came to beauty, it was not enough simply to admire something on an intellectual level; instead, it had to elicit a deep emotional response. They believed that artists should be totally free to create whatever they wished, often using pastoral themes and those of nature. For followers of the movement, the focus on enlightenment and the rush to rationalise every aspect of the natural world was creating a society that looked no further than its cities and factories.

In its obsession with modernisation, society was losing touch with the power and wonder of nature, so Romantics emphasised the importance of spending time away from urban landscapes and all their constructed distractions; by spending time in nature, they believed, a person might truly discover what beauty and truth was.

By the time of the Regency era, the Romantic movement was firmly entrenched and enormously popular. From the beginning of the Romantic period in the 18th century, landscape art that reflected the movement often captured wild scenes and violent storms, rather than simple bucolic landscapes, which were at the time considered a somewhat low form of art. It was these early examples of the movement that were to influence the artists who became celebrated during the Regency era.

John Constable was one of the first Romantic artists to eschew the vogue for idealising landscapes, and to instead paint directly from reality. In doing so, he pioneered the Naturalism movement, bringing to life the world exactly as he saw it. He took his inspiration not from the Romantic's favourite subject of dramatic

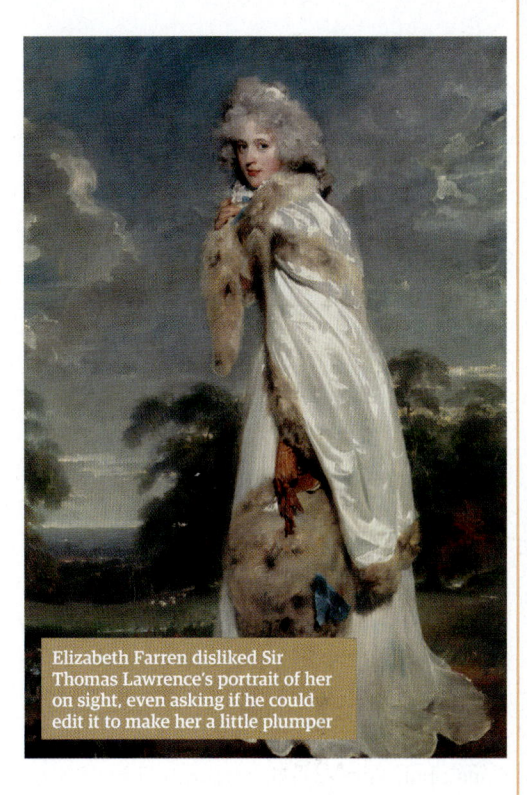

Elizabeth Farren disliked Sir Thomas Lawrence's portrait of her on sight, even asking if he could edit it to make her a little plumper

"It was not enough simply to admire something on an intellectual level; it had to elicit a deep emotional response"

Turner's daunting depiction of Hannibal crossing the Alps captures the men beneath a terrifying storm cloud as an avalanche descends, with a pale sun their only hope of salvation

107

CULTURE & KNOWLEDGE

mountains, but from the landscapes he had known since childhood. Though Constable took up portrait painting in order to pay his bills, he found the work stifling, despite enjoying great acclaim. Instead, he preferred to be among the people and landscapes he knew best, creating works that celebrated the British landscape and the people who lived and worked in it, producing such celebrated works as *The Hay Wain*.

Just as Constable made his name as a landscape painter, JMW Turner rose to prominence for his dramatic and often turbulent seascapes. Known for his remarkable adeptness with colour, Turner became known as 'the painter of light'. Like Constable, he emphasised the dramatic impact of natural light, capturing it dynamically on the canvas. There was no effort to idealise the image, but instead to capture it in its natural splendour, fury and beauty. When he turned his hand to history painting, such as his *Snow Storm: Hannibal and His army Crossing the Alps*, the work was brought to life by the light and landscape – in the case of this painting, it glowers over and dwarfs the tiny figures below. In Turner's hands, light could change the emotion of a landscape or render a mundane scene breathtaking. Little wonder, then, that he soon found himself in great demand among the upper classes, who hoped that he might capture their grandest homes in a painting and imbue them with a little of his magic.

It's little wonder that the vain Prince Regent adored Sir Thomas Lawrence, who depicted him as stately and imposing in his Garter robes

Once exhibited as a novelty, Sarah Biffen became a celebrated painter of miniatures and eventually received a pension from Queen Victoria

108

The Prince Regent, of course, was one of the era's greatest tastemakers and he was a particular fan of the works of Sir Thomas Lawrence, who was famed for his portraiture. Arguably it is Lawrence, more than any other artist, who has shaped our visual image of the Regency period and as Principal Painter in Ordinary to the King, he was in great demand among the era's most important figures. Lawrence led the way in Regency portraits, lending his male sitters a brooding swagger and imparting his female subjects with a knowing beauty. Moving as he did in fashionable society, Lawrence brought something of the character of his sitters into their portraits and he approached their clothing and accessories with the same amount of care as he did their faces. Often posed against dramatic backdrops, a Lawrence portrait is rich in texture and colour, filled with life and splendour. It is no surprise that he became the most fashionable and popular portraitist in Europe. Even now, his subjects look as though they might step out of their frames.

While Lawrence may have apparently cornered the market when it came to portraits, Charlotte Jones enjoyed the prestigious position of Miniature Painter to Princess Charlotte of Wales. She produced delicate miniatures for her patron, the daughter of the Prince Regent, and her work soon brought her to the attention of the upper classes and other members of the royal family. Jones painted an early portrait of the Duke of Clarence, later to reign as William IV, as well a portrait of the Prince Regent himself.

However, Jones's most celebrated work is a triptych made up of a dozen portraits of Princess Charlotte, which was painted after the princess's death at the age of 21. Jones's work memorialised Charlotte's life from cradle to grave and became a treasured part of the Royal Collection.

Also celebrated for her miniatures, Anne Mee had gained royal patronage when she was commissioned to paint portraits of the daughters of King George III and later Princess Charlotte of Wales. However, Mee also had a very particular niche: she painted miniature portraits of society beauties from the reign of George III. Few people loved a society beauty more than the Prince Regent, who commissioned her to paint portraits of his favourite fashionable beauties. The paintings were then sent to Windsor for the Prince's personal enjoyment.

Rising to prominence during the Regency period, Sarah Biffin was born without arms and only vestigial legs. Painting using her mouth, she spent her early years being exhibited as an attraction until she attracted the patronage of the Earl of Morton, who financed her training and brought her to prominence in society. Initially regarded as something of a novelty, Biffen's very real talent soon established her as a miniaturist of renown, and she was commissioned by the royal household to produce miniatures of the royal family. Her studio in Bond Street went on to become a place of pilgrimage for the great and the good, all desperate to employ her talents.

The artistic record that remains of the Regency era contains some of the most famed and revered names in British painting. Though undoubtedly the preserve of male artists above female, it was a time when Romanticism dominated, and the upper classes and tastemakers embraced those who followed it. Where the Prince Regent trod, the fashionable and influential quickly followed, eager to reflect the Prince's taste and hopefully win his favour. In a time when splendour and brilliance was celebrated and held dear, art could be used to build a personal myth, to celebrate the grandeur and status of one person, or to elevate a humble corner of pastoral England to mythical status. It truly was a time like no other.

By Charlotte Jones, the eye of Princess Charlotte of Wales is set in a memorial locket and contains a lock of the late princess's own hair

> "The Regency era contains some of the most revered names in British painting"

Élisabeth Vigée Le Brun

A celebrated artistic daughter of France visited England before the Regency era, to great acclaim

In 1802, Élisabeth Vigée Le Brun visited England and stayed for three years, rejuvenating a career that the French Revolution had almost destroyed. Le Brun had established herself at the Court of Versailles by the age of 20 and became Marie Antoinette's favourite painter. She produced 30 portraits of the queen before, in 1789, she found herself the victim of a campaign of slander for her closeness to Marie Antoinette. Fearing what the future might hold, Le Brun left her husband, fled France and went into exile with her daughter, Julie.

During her time in exile in Europe, Le Brun found that her romantic portraits perfectly captured the prevailing mood, and her career flourished. At first, when she arrived in England, Le Brun found the country stuffy and lifeless, but she immersed herself in the artistic landscape, visiting the studios of her contemporaries. She became a fashionable salon hostess but never truly settled into the country, which seemed to her very different from the continent. Spurred on by her memories of the homeland she had adored, Le Brun left England to return to France, and a commission to paint Caroline Bonaparte, sister of the Emperor Napoleon.

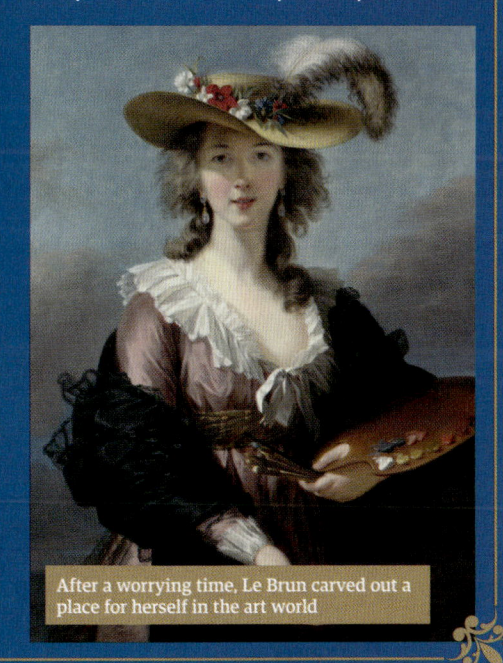

After a worrying time, Le Brun carved out a place for herself in the art world

CULTURE & KNOWLEDGE

THE GRAND TOUR

In the 17th and 18th centuries, hordes of young aristocrats journeyed across the continent, seeking to expand their knowledge of art and antiquity

WRITTEN BY **CALLUM MCKELVIE**

Katharine Read's 1750 depiction of a group of young English tourists in Rome

For almost two centuries, the Grand Tour was deemed an integral part of a young gentleman's education. During the 17th and to early 19th centuries, the sons of Britain's elite were shipped to the European continent for a period lasting from months to years. The intention was for the young man in question to gain a greater understanding of classical art, architecture and culture by experiencing it first hand. They would also be expected to return home with souvenirs of their trip, demonstrating their new-found taste as well as providing evidence of their having completed this most important rite of passage.

ORIGINS OF THE GRAND TOUR

The Grand Tour is considered to have its origins in 1613 and a journey made by the architect Inigo Jones, who travelled to Italy, visiting cities such as Naples and Rome. The architecture he witnessed while on this trip profoundly influenced him and when he was appointed the Surveyor of the King's Works in 1615, Jones drew heavily on classical styles. Structures such as the Banqueting House, Whitehall best exemplify the influence of Roman architecture on Jones's own work.

But this influence quickly spread beyond Jones alone and the introduction of these continental styles fundamentally changed British architecture, eventually sparking a neoclassical revolution. Furthermore, others were themselves entranced by the antiquarian world that had inspired Jones and embarked on trips of their own. Soon, a first-

CULTURE & KNOWLEDGE

hand knowledge of classical culture began to be seen as an important final part of a young gentleman's education.

It was in 1670 that Richard Lassels coined the term, 'Grand Tour' in his *A Voyage of Italy*, considered one of the first guidebooks. In it, Lassels outlined his ideas that such journeys were integral to the education of young gentlemen, who hungrily devoured Lassels' work as one of the view available books on the subject. Lassels himself became known as something of an expert on Italy, acting as a 'bear leader' for many of the affluent youths who travelled there.

WHO TOOK THE GRAND TOUR?
As previously stated, the Grand Tourists were mostly the young sons of wealthy families. These young men could be anywhere between the ages of 17 and 22, though in most cases were around the age of 21. Although the Grand Tour was not limited purely to British travellers, it is with Britain that the phenomenon is primarily associated. Despite some travelling for shorter periods, most tourists would usually be away from home for at least a year.

These journeys were no easy task, particularly in the early years of the phenomenon. In her 2008 paper on the Grand Tour for the architectural journal *Perspecta*, Gillian Darley stated some of the difficulties encountered in these early tours; "Entry controls were time consuming and officials fraudulent; even the actual location of borders could be unpredictable. Once on the road, there were incomprehensible dialects to confuse the best-prepared linguist, as well as the oddities in diet, currency, and, above all, religion."

WHAT HAPPENED ON THE GRAND TOUR?
But just what were these hordes of young aristocrats doing as they flocked to the continent? Typically accompanied by a tutor, referred to as a 'bear leader', they would spend much of their time travelling to ruins and contemplating the majesty of the ancient world. They may have also viewed the masterpieces of the Renaissance, building an understanding not only of classical antiquity but more contemporary culture. Particularly well-connected travellers might spend time at court, mingling with high society and learning etiquette.

But for some of these young men, their diaries reveal that the main highlight of the trip was of a more hedonistic nature. "What they tended to do was to go and drink a lot, to gamble, to frequent [sex workers]" Eric G Zuelow, the author of *A History of Modern Tourism*, told the ABC *Rear Vision* podcast. This behaviour did not go unnoticed, with many returning having contracted venereal diseases or having incurred huge losses from gambling. Surgeon Samuel Sharp, just one critic of the Grand Tour, publicly condemned what he perceived as the morally corrupting nature of the Italian culture, in his 1766 work, *Letters From Italy*.

ABOVE LEFT Thomas Rowlandson's 1767 caricature, *Englishman at Paris*, mocking the way the 18th century tourist was viewed by Parisian locals

TOP A group of Grand Tourists visit the ruins of Pompey in the early 19th century

ABOVE The temple ruins at Paestum, c 1785. The ruins were a popular spot among Grand Tourists

LEFT An example of an 18th century architectural model, of the kind commissioned by Grand Tourists

But for others, the trip provided a freedom from the constricting laws of British society. Author Jeremy Black states that Britain in the 18th century had seen a hardening of attitudes towards homosexuality, whereas Italy provided young gay men seeking to explore their sexuality with a veritable playground in which to do so. Famed poet Lord Byron undertook his own Grand Tour in the Mediterranean in 1809, purportedly having a number of troubling relationships with adolescent boys.

WHERE DID THEY GO?
Most Grand Tourists would begin their journey in Dover, taking a three-day voyage across the Channel until they arrived in France, where they would likely spend some time in Paris. At the time the city was a highly fashionable destination, renowned for its fine art and culture. According to Arturo Tosi in his 2020 work, *Language and the Grand Tour*, "most visitors were acquainted with only two itineraries in France; from the border to Paris, and from Paris to Italy".

However, the main destination was Italy and historic cities such as Rome, Naples, Florence and Venice. But in order to arrive in Italy, how did the Grand Tourists cross the Alps? One popular way of making the

THE GRAND TOUR

journey was by sedan chair, which was a chair in the middle of a pair of poles, carried by local guides. "They are light, & well contrived for carrying," Grand Tourist Sir William Guise wrote in a diary entry from 1764. "You take 4 or 6 men, who change at fixed distances, and carry you an amazing pace."

COLLECTING SOUVENIRS

One of the most important aspects of the Grand Tour was the collecting of souvenirs. The nature of these souvenirs could vary wildly and included everything from original Italian antiquities – taken from historical sites – to paintings, to bound books. These treasures were not merely mementos, but were intended to function as status symbols that proved their owners to be widely travelled and highly cultured. Many took the opportunity to have their portraits painted, with the skills of the famous artist Pompeo Batoni being the most sought after.

The Grand Tour also saw the rise in an entirely new industry. These young wealthy travellers, touched by the works they had seen, began to commission artists to create replicas for their homes – leading to the rise of the replica tourism industry.

In the 18th century, architectural replicas of ancient ruins made out of cork

ABOVE *The Tribuna of the Uffizi* by Johann Zoffany, a depiction of the famous collection of the Duke of Tuscany in Florence

ABOVE RIGHT Lady Mary Wortley Montagu who travelled to Italy and eventually moved there permanently

proved popular when it was discovered that this unassuming material could properly capture the texture of ancient, crumbling marble. Others soon began to make their own miniature cork marvels, such as Augusto Rosa, Antonio Chichi and Giovanni Altieri. Commissioned through art dealers, they created tiny replicas of ancient marvels such as the Doric temples at Paestum, the Colosseum and the Temple of Vesta at Tivoli.

END OF THE GRAND TOUR

By the early 1900s, the Grand Tour had already started to become a thing of the past. There were a variety of reasons for this. Over a century earlier, in 1789, France was rocked by revolution and four years later Louis XVI and his bride, Marie Antoinette, would be executed. Although this monumental event did not immediately cause the Grand Tours to cease, it made travel much more difficult and was the beginning of the end. However, the most damning blow was the opening of the first passenger rail service in 1807. By the mid-19th century, the railway had become a popular form of transportation across Europe. The result was, while travel was still predominantly a luxury for the upper classes, it was becoming far more commonplace.

Women on the Grand Tour

Contrary to popular belief, it wasn't just the boys who went away to have some fun on the continent...

Although the Grand Tour is often thought of as being a predominantly male experience, many women also embarked upon travels of their own. Usually this would be to accompany their husband or another relative, particularly as travel across the continent became more popular. According to Rosemary Sweet's *Cities and the Grand Tour*, as time wore on mothers and fathers would take their daughters there to complete their own educations and gain a wider appreciation of art and culture. Mary Wollstonecraft, the celebrated women's rights activist, was one of the few who were able to travel abroad as part of her education.

But this was not always the case and there are examples of women taking journeys unaccompanied. In 1739, Lady Mary Wortley Montagu travelled to Italy, leaving her husband in pursuit of a young lover, only to be jilted upon her arrival. It wasn't a loss – she found herself falling in love with the country. She eventually moved there permanently and her adoration for her new home was well known. According to Rosemary Sweet, in 1794 Sarah Bentham claimed to have met an "otherwise unidentified Mrs Motte" who "travelled on her own accompanied by her female servant".

CULTURE & KNOWLEDGE

Take a trip...

Paris
Charles Grevenbroeck's 1741 depiction of Paris

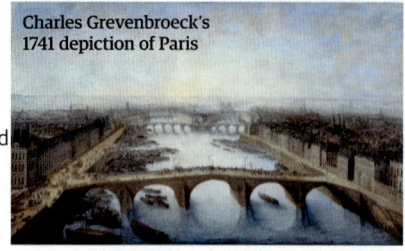

Paris was one of the most popular stops on the Grand Tour and at the time was considered the height of modern society. Most young English aristocrats would have spoken French, so the city provided them with an opportunity to test their linguistic skills. The city was also where the young men could be expected to learn the manners of high society.

Geneva
A 18th century depiction of the famous view over the lake

Before crossing the Alps the Grand Tourist would usually stop in Switzerland in either Geneva or Lausanne. The famous lake proved a popular spot to while away the hours, but many of the young men were unimpressed with the locals. Horace Walpole in 1739 noted, "Such uncouth rocks and such uncomely inhabitants... I hope I shall never see them again".

Turin
Bernardo Bellotto's bridge over the river Po in Turin

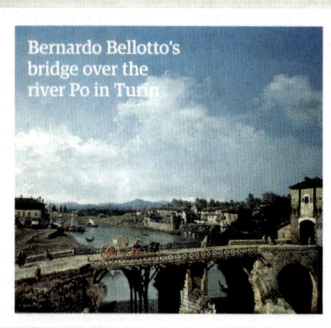

Turin was viewed as 'the gateway to Italy'. Some would stay and enjoy the natural beauty on offer, whereas others would quickly move on. Particularly aristocratic travellers may have found themselves presented at the court of Savoy, where they would have had the perfect opportunity to refine their etiquette.

Florence

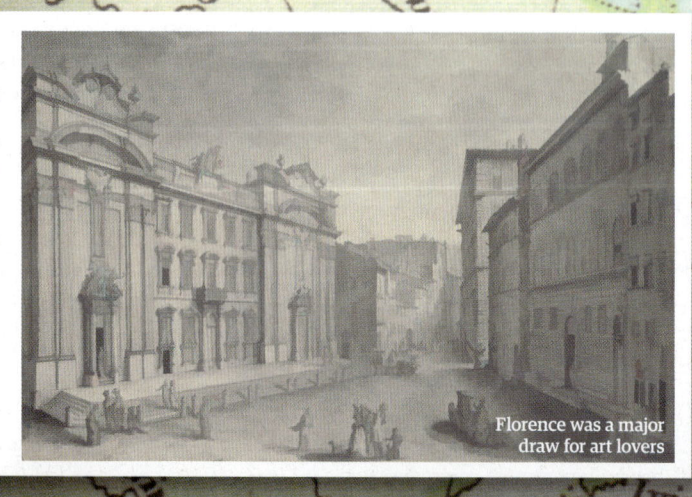

Florence was known for its art. In particular the Tribuna in the Uffizi Gallery, which housed the Duke of Tuscany's vast collection of famous masterworks of the Italian Renaissance, was a must visit for any Grand Tourist. By the 19th century a significant British community had emerged in the city.

Florence was a major draw for art lovers

THE GRAND TOUR

Fancy expanding your knowledge of classical antiquity or brushing up on your courtly manners? Follow the Grand Tour route…

Venice

Venice provided inspiration and venereal disease!

The beauty of Venice, particularly the canals, entranced the Grand Tourists and saw a number of landscape souvenirs commissioned by them. Venice was also known as a hive of vice and decadence, notorious for its many brothels, where a number of young men visited and returned with strains of venereal disease.

Vienna

Jean Pelletier's View of the Ponte Santa Trinita Across the Arno River

Although Naples was primarily viewed as the tour's conclusion, Grand Tourists might choose to take a brief sojourn at a European city on the journey home. From the 1750s onwards, Vienna was increasingly popular for this. It was viewed as somewhere where courtly manners could be learnt and was known for education and culture.

Rome

Lord Byron depicted contemplating the Colosseum. Byron completed his own Grand Tour in 1809

Rome was considered the principal destination for many a Grand Tourist. This stop would be one of study and pleasure, with the tourists visiting historical ruins such as the Forum and Colosseum as well as viewing the many art treasures the city had to offer. A popular souvenir from the city was a portrait by Pompeo Batoni.

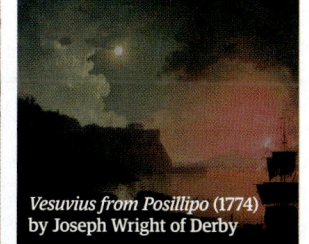

Naples

Vesuvius from Posillipo (1774) by Joseph Wright of Derby

The discovery of Pompeii towards the end of the 16th century made Naples a popular destination. The city also became popular for the cultural entertainment it offered, namely the opera. Some brave travellers would even attempt the difficult ascent of Mount Vesuvius.

CULTURE & KNOWLEDGE

A tour of REGENCY ENGLAND

Follow in the footsteps of the Prince Regent and Jane Austen on our guided tour of their most-loved locations

WRITTEN BY **SCOTT REEVES**

If Tripadvisor existed in 1815, its top ten places to see would inevitably focus on London. The British capital was where the great and the good of the Regency era spent most of their time. Unfortunately, some of the period's finest buildings are no longer with us. The Prince Regent's opulent London home, Carlton House, didn't long survive his accession to the throne. Astley's Amphitheatre, an extravagant entertainment arena in Lambeth, has also disappeared under modern development. But plenty of highlights are still with us. From parks for pleasure to royal residences, this is our selection of the places to go to capture the spirit of the Regency era.

This unusual view of Buckingham Palace shows it with Marble Arch still in its original position

BUCKINGHAM PALACE
London

Although more commonly associated with Queens Victoria and Elizabeth II, Buckingham Palace's status as a royal residence began under King George IV. After taking the throne in 1820, he commissioned John Nash to overhaul Queen Charlotte's old residence, Buckingham House. Nash's instructions were to build new wings around a central courtyard and a French Neoclassical façade facing The Mall. The new-look palace included Marble Arch, a grand ceremonial entrance, although that was moved in 1851 to make way for a new East Range. The expensive renovation spiralled out of control and Nash was sacked as the cost reached £500,000. Progress was slow, and the new palace wasn't finished before King George died in 1830. His vision eventually became a reality, however, and Queen Victoria made Buckingham Palace her primary home upon her accession in 1837.

A TOUR OF REGENCY ENGLAND

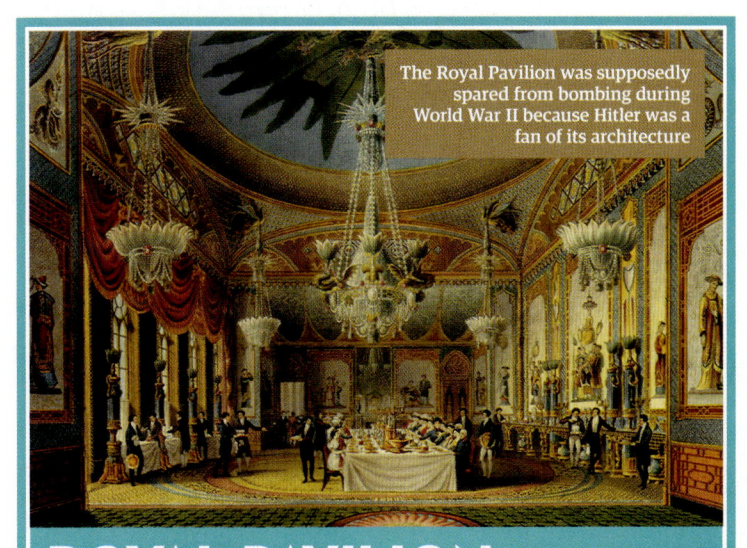

The Royal Pavilion was supposedly spared from bombing during World War II because Hitler was a fan of its architecture

ROYAL PAVILION
Brighton

George, Prince of Wales, first visited Brighton in 1783 at the age of 21. In theory, the fresh air and seawater was supposed to help his gout. In reality, George used Brighton as a hedonistic playground and fed his vices. The Prince stayed with his uncle, the Duke of Cumberland, who shared George's tastes for gambling, nightlife and women. Brighton's distance from London also made it a discreet place to meet his Catholic lover, Maria Fitzherbert. By 1787, Prince George decided to build a place of his own. He rented a modest farmhouse facing the promenade and set about transforming it beyond recognition. He added a new wing and central rotunda containing a breakfast room, dining room and library.

Subsequent additions enlarged the Pavilion and added new rooms, while a major refurbishment under John Nash between 1815 and 1822 made the Royal Pavilion we know today. The design of the Pavilion reflected Britain's growing empire. It's Indo-Islamic exterior included domes and minarets, while the interior decoration took the Prince's visitors on an international tour through China, India and Persia. Queen Victoria wasn't a fan, however, and she sold the Pavilion to Brighton Council.

THEATRE ROYAL
London

The Theatre Royal had a troubled history. An assassin fired two pistol shots at King George III there in 1800, and it burned down in 1809. That didn't stop a new theatre rising from the ashes, and the Regency-era building hosted its first performance - a production of *Hamlet* - in 1812. It gained a reputation for elaborate staging and special effects, and the theatre now hosts West End shows including *Charlie and the Chocolate Factory*.

VAUXHALL GARDENS
London

Commercial pleasure gardens were the theme parks of the Regency era. Guests paid a fee to enter the privately-owned parks, where they'd be entertained by musicians and performers. Some included assembly rooms or concert halls to shelter in if the weather turned bad, but the main reason for visiting was to see and be seen. Eligible bachelors and debutantes dressed in their finest garments and strolled the paths between immaculate flowerbeds. Vauxhall Gardens gained a reputation as the capital's premier pleasure garden with its special events including hot-air balloon ascents, firework displays and battle reenactments. Most guests arrived after 5pm and the last left in the early hours. Although the gardens were lit with gas lamps, pickpockets were common and guests had to keep a close eye on their valuables.

Anybody was welcome to a pleasure garden as long as they were respectably dressed and could afford the entrance fee

PITTVILLE
Cheltenham

The growing spa town of Cheltenham got the royal seal of approval when King George III and Queen Charlotte visited in 1788. Local speculator Joseph Pitt saw the opportunity to make some money. He bought land north of the town and began building an entirely new settlement. Pittville, as he called it, was intended to be an upmarket resort of 600 houses surrounded by parklands and pleasure gardens. The centrepiece was Pittville Park, featuring long paths for riding and walking. Access to the park was restricted to residents and visitors to the Pump Room, a grand building fronted by Ionic columns. Inside, a marble and plaster water pump dispensed natural spring water and a ballroom hosted evening events. Pittville lost its independence as Cheltenham expanded, but its Regency-era architecture still survives today.

The property market slumped during the building of Pittville and only 20 houses had been finished when the Pump Room opened

117

CULTURE & KNOWLEDGE

THE COBB
Lyme Regis

The Dorset town of Lyme Regis became a fashionable seaside resort at the turn of the 19th century thanks to a 500-year-old harbour wall. The Cobb, as the stone storm break was known, was adopted by Regency-era tourists as a bracing sea walk. Among the visitors who ambled to its end was Jane Austen, who visited in 1803 and 1804. While in Lyme Regis, Austen also used bathing machines on the beach. These clever machines enabled respectable men and women to change into swimwear and take a dip in the sea without revealing themselves to onlookers. Austen must have enjoyed her trips to Lyme Regis, because the Cobb features in her novel *Persuasion* – although modern visitors are encouraged not to follow her character's example by jumping off the wall.

The Cobb was a popular place for artists who were seeking inspiration

GRAND PUMP ROOM
Bath

Bath had long been known for its restorative spa waters – after all, the Romans built an entire town around them – but it was during the Regency period that the town transformed into a social hub second only to London. Visitors flocked to Somerset to take the waters at the Grand Pump Room, an elegant chamber built above the old Roman baths. The daily gathering in the impressive, open room was a place to exchange news and gossip while imbibing the rejuvenating but egg-scented water. Today, the Pump Room has been converted into a grand restaurant. Those in search of a lighter lunch should take the short walk to Sally Lunn's for a sweet bread that was a favourite treat in Regency era.

Sick and ill people would travel from all over to drink Bath's egg-scented water

WHITE'S
London

The raucous atmosphere at White's was featured in William Hogarth's prints

As the premier gentlemen's club in London, White's was a place where the great and the good could eat, drink, and most importantly, gamble – an activity that was illegal outside private clubs. It wasn't easy to gain entry, though. White's used a system of voting for prospective members whereby white and black balls were dropped into a bag. A single no-vote cast using a black ball was enough to deny membership, hence the term 'being blackballed'. One lucky man who was accepted into White's was fashionista Beau Brummell. He'd sit in the bow window of the club passing judgement on the appearances of those walking by. White's is still one of the most exclusive clubs in London, with King Charles III and Prince William among its members, although not their wives – White's still retains its men-only rule.

118

A TOUR OF REGENCY ENGLAND

REGENT'S PARK
London

The woodland on what was then London's outskirts came into the possession of the Crown during the dissolution of the monasteries, and generations of monarchs used it as a private hunting ground. The Prince Regent had other ideas, however. By 1810, the land was enclosed by London's urban sprawl, and George decided to redevelop it as a pleasure garden. He didn't intend to pay for it himself, however. Instead, property developer James Burton stepped in and took charge of the project. He fronted most of the cost and commissioned John Nash to design the new gardens. He also laid out the streets around the park, all named for members of the royal family.

At first, access to the park was restricted to the wealthy residents of the new houses. They should have been joined by the Prince Regent, who wanted a summer palace built in the park for his own use, but rising costs meant that construction of that building never started. The processional way leading to the unbuilt palace was constructed, and it survives today as Regent Street. London Zoo took up residence in a corner of the park in 1828, and the rest of Regent's Park was opened to the public in 1835.

AN ISLAND ON THE LAKE & PART OF CORNWALL & CLARENCE TERRACE, REGENT'S PARK.

Aside from ornamental lakes, Regent's Park also features a canal linking the Grand Union Canal to the River Thames

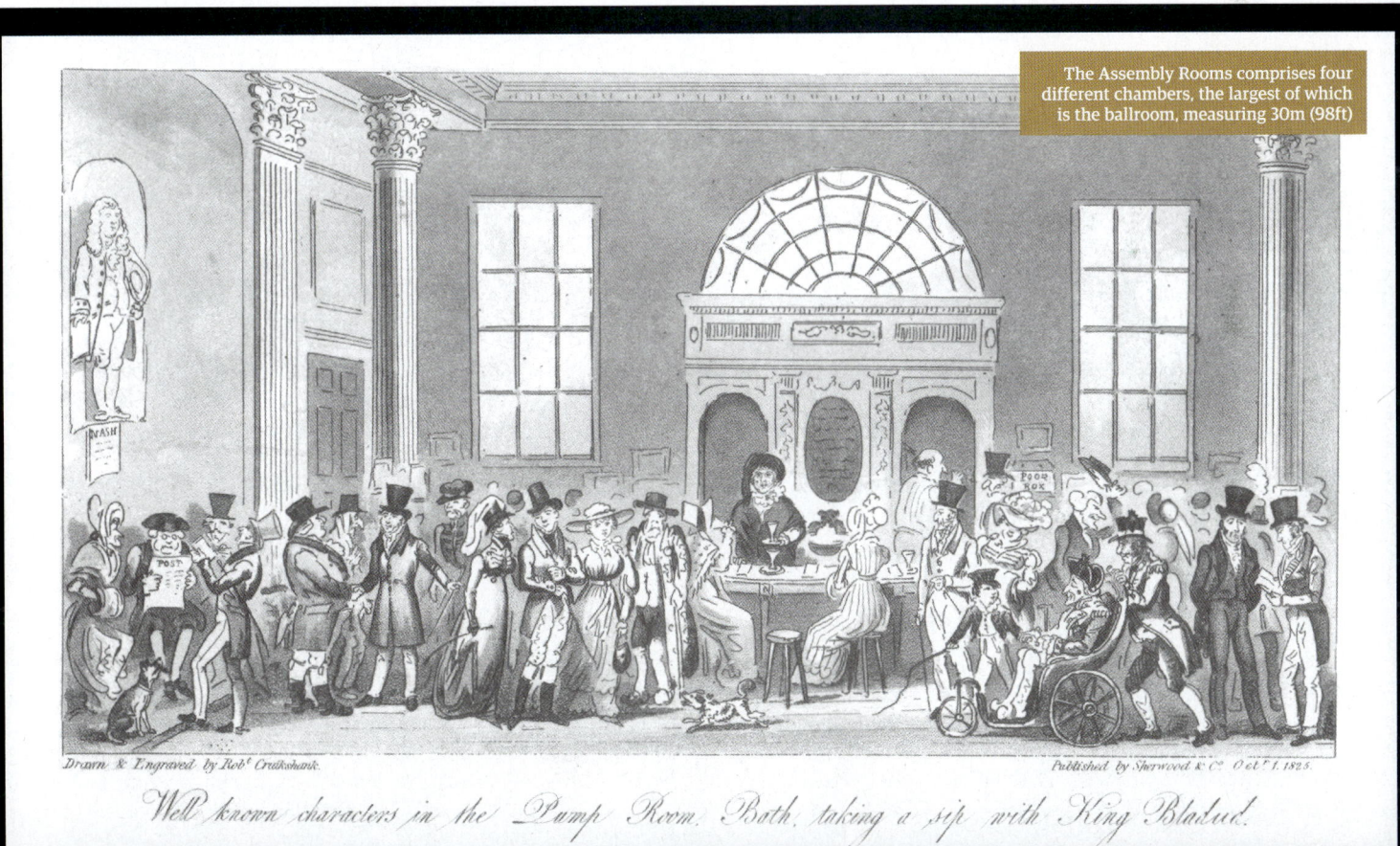

The Assembly Rooms comprises four different chambers, the largest of which is the ballroom, measuring 30m (98ft)

Well known characters in the Pump Room, Bath, taking a sip with King Bladud.

ASSEMBLY ROOMS
Bath

Bath's booming popularity as a social destination meant that the old Assembly Rooms built early in the 18th century weren't big enough to hold the crowds. Architect John Wood the Younger plugged the gap with the new Assembly Rooms. They opened in 1771 with a grand ball, and afterwards played host to two balls a week. On other nights, people used the rooms to play cards, listen to musicians and take tea. Guests included Jane Austen, who lived in Bath for four years and would have been a regular patron. She used the Assembly Rooms as a backdrop in both *Persuasion* and *Northanger Abbey*. The Assembly Rooms are now owned by the National Trust and retain just as much glamour as ever.

CULTURE & KNOWLEDGE

By the end of the Industrial Revolution, trains were hastening the growth of industry and export across the Empire

THE INDUSTRIAL REVOLUTION

A new technological age dawned with the Industrial Revolution, bringing wealth for some and deprivation for others

WRITTEN BY **CATHERINE CURZON**

Throughout the 18th century and into the 19th, the United Kingdom expanded at a rapid rate as the reach of the Empire spread around the globe. This unprecedented expansion meant that there was an increased demand for goods. In a world where the vast majority of manufacturing was still done by hand and rural and agricultural industries prevailed, large-scale heavy industry became vital to the continued supply and expansion of the kingdom.

At first technological growth was necessarily slow due to the natural limits imposed by the available technologies such as windmills or waterwheels, while transport across the country was confined to the horse on land or boats on water. The Industrial Revolution changed all that and it began with textiles, one of the country's most valuable manufacturing sectors. In this vital industry, once change began, it was swift indeed.

Textile production was one of the country's most important industries and it was a magnet for entrepreneurs and inventors, all of them keen to speed up the process and maximise profits. In the 18th century innovations such as James Hargreave's spinning jenny and Richard Arkwright's water frame, which completely removed the need for wool or linen in weaving, allowed work that had once taken a whole team to be done by a single machine. These innovations were combined by Samuel Crompton into the spinning mule, which produced a thread of then unparalleled strength and quality.

Each of these new developments took textile production one step further away from the cottage industry it had once been and as the industry developed, so too did the roles of the men and women who worked in it. Though small-scale spinning had often been done by women, the operation of machines such as the mule needed brute force and responsibility for this passed to men. Women took over the operation of looms instead, freeing the men to work the mules.

The shift towards large-scale textile manufacture laid the foundations of the Industrial Revolution but when James Watt and Matthew Boulton patented their steam engine in 1775, the result was an unprecedented leap forward. Initially used in the mining industry for pumping water, steam power brought automation to factories that would once have relied on water for power. Factories could now be built away from water sources for the first time, powered instead by steam. This point was driven home by the opening of Shudehill Mill in 1783. This centre of manufacturing was nowhere near a water source and stood at Manchester's highest point, looking out over the so-called Cottonopolis.

Opened in 1781, Shropshire's Iron Bridge was celebrated as the first to be made of cast iron

"Canal-building technologies completely reshaped the country's network of inland water transport"

In the inferno-like ironworks, the Industrial Revolution opened up a whole new world of progress. The introduction of a process known as puddling in the late 1700s meant that strong iron could now be mass produced in England for the first time and metal parts for the machines that powered the Industrial Revolution could be made efficiently, quickly and economically. As steam engines improved coal mining, the supply of coal became seemingly endless and it was more affordable than ever. This in turn fed into the iron industry, creating the perfect combination of industries working in tandem. The United Kingdom no longer needed to import and pay for iron but instead began to export and profit from it instead. Just as Manchester grew rich on cotton, now the West Midlands became famed as the Black Country, sitting as it did at the very centre of the metalworking industry.

The need to bring all of these industrial elements together to improve efficiency meant that manufacturing moved into towns and cities, where vast factories centralised production under one roof. Though geographical areas had their own specialities, these became industrial in nature. The once flourishing world of cottage production was slowly dying, becoming smothered by mass production.

Yet all of this innovation was of little use if the products manufactured in the factories couldn't be transported to their consumers at more than a snail's pace. The first innovation in transport came with the creation of a new canal system, which crisscrossed the land and allowed for the speedy transportation of manufactured goods. Britain's canal network underwent a complete overhaul and programme of modernisation, allowing for the efficient transportation of all manner of goods between key industrial centres and beyond.

Canal-building technologies completely reshaped the country's network of inland water transport. Though early canals couldn't go uphill and instead had to find a way around the landscape, modern locks enabled canal transport to easily climb hills, while advancements in tunnel building and aqueduct construction took canals into places where they couldn't have been laid before.

Later still, the earliest railways brought new innovation and possibilities for industrial growth, long before the internal combustion engine did. Suddenly transport was faster than it had ever been, sending British goods to the furthest corners of the United Kingdom and far beyond.

Steam, which had revolutionised so much of the industrial world, made the burgeoning export industry wealthier than ever. Cities such as Newcastle and Liverpool became the centre of the maritime world, with shipbuilding yards supplying the expanding docks. The improved availability and lower cost of iron and steel allowed for more robust vessels and steamships were the perfect solution to continue the growth of United Kingdom export, shipping British goods all over the world and bringing more money than ever into the economy.

Yet it wasn't only in water transport that things were changing. Thanks to the likes of John Loudon McAdam, who pioneered a technique of constructing roads called 'macadamisation', the nation's roads were also improving. In 1816, surveyor McAdam began to replace the Bristol

Huge mills such as the one at Cromford made entrepreneurs like Richard Arkwright rich men

THE INDUSTRIAL REVOLUTION

A vast canal network enabled efficient transport of the raw materials needed for manufacturing, not to mention finished goods

James Hargreaves' spinning jenny revolutionised weaving, reducing the time and labour needed to produce cloth

Steam engines like those designed by James Watt were the driving force behind the Industrial Revolution

A revolution in working conditions

Working conditions during the Industrial Revolution were far from ideal and with workers flocking to the cities in huge numbers, employers exploited their availability to pay as little as they possibly dared. Workers were forced to endure unimaginably long days in hazardous conditions in return for a pittance. After all, few factory owners wanted to dent their profits by paying a decent wage.

In the hulking monoliths that housed British industry, workers toiled in conditions that could be shocking. With little light and often in extreme temperatures, they kept the wheels of industry turning.

For all their importance as the people who actually operated the means of production, workers during the Industrial Revolution enjoyed precious few rights. They were considered to be near the very bottom of the social heap and for every responsible captain of industry who looked out for his workers, there were plenty who barely saw them as more than machines themselves. As a result, workers began to organise into what became the first labour unions. They campaigned for a fair day's pay as well as the promise that they would be able to work without facing the very real danger of injury, for which they could expect to receive nothing in the way of compensation.

Very slowly, government started responding to the calls for better conditions. Limits were eventually put on working hours, initially for children, then for women, but the pace of change was still slow and for the workers of Britain, life was destined to be hard for many years to come.

As the 18th century progressed, British workers began to organise themselves in the hope of gaining better rights and working conditions

roads under his care with a new surface that he had developed. A covering of tightly compacted crushed stones was employed on raised roads, creating a surface that was less susceptible to rainwater and was considered the most significant leap forward in road technology in centuries. This meant that the arduous journey from London to Edinburgh, which had taken a fortnight in approximately 1800, could be completed in as little as two days just 30 years later.

In this brave new world of industry, no other nation could compete with Britain's ability to turn out what was needed, when it was needed.

Although the pace of change wasn't overnight, urban areas began to slowly replace the more scattered communities that had once powered the rural and cottage industries. Cities and towns became the centre of manufacturing and people moved from smaller areas into urban centres, to be closer than ever to their places of work. This meant that there was a necessary expansion of public spaces in towns and cities, to ensure that these new inhabitants had places not only to work, but to play, worship and shop, too.

In the changing world, the rewards for those at the top of the pile were immense. Banking flourished in the face of so much new wealth and as the Georgian era gave way to the Victorians in 1837, the first commercial electrical telegraph was bring patented by English duo William Cooke and Charles Wheatstone.

Yet for those who toiled in the factories to make all of these revolutionary dreams a reality, things weren't always so comfortable. Children joined their parents working in difficult and often dangerous positions and women, who had once been the heart of the home, now became another cog in the industrial machine. They worked alongside the men, performing tasks that were just as laborious, yet receiving less money than their male counterparts.

Over the course of decades, the Industrial Revolution changed the face of Britain in every sense of the word. Once an island nation powered by small-scale agricultural and agrarian industry, the country became the centre of a changing world and the heart of an expanding empire. It was a time of unmatched growth and prosperity for some, and punishing upheaval for others. The modern age was dawning and with it, the United Kingdom was discovering what it meant to be the Workshop of the World.

CULTURE & KNOWLEDGE

DOCTOR'S ORDERS

Step into the waiting room and uncover the brutal treatments on offer to the sick

WRITTEN BY **SCOTT REEVES**

When Frances Burney felt a lump in her breast in 1810, her heart sank. She knew it was a sign that there could be something seriously wrong. Physicians confirmed her worst fear: breast cancer. They advised her to have the lump removed in an operation, but Burney wasn't keen to go under the knife – and for good reason.

Over the next few decades, medics would make major breakthroughs in the study of medicine – but that was all in the future when Burney discovered her lump. In the Regency era, there were no anaesthetics and antiseptics to make surgery safer. There were no X-rays to see inside the body without cutting it open. Instead, Burney underwent a tortuous 20-minute operation with nothing more than a cup of wine to dull the pain and a number of heavyset men to hold her down.

Burney's nightmare experience was nothing unusual. At the turn of the 19th century, medical knowledge was more medieval than modern. The prevailing belief was that illness and disease was caused by bad air, or 'miasma'. Rotting flesh and filth created a bad smell, and doctors believed that breathing in the stench would cause a person to fall ill themselves.

So the best way to avoid falling ill was to avoid bad air. Both men and women would carry fresh flowers and perfumed handkerchiefs to cover their nose and mouth if they stumbled across a foul miasma. Since miasmas were thought to be more

Apothecaries were the cheapest way for patients to access treatment, although many cures did more harm than good

At a time before anaesthetics and antiseptics, surgery was the last resort

> "Medical knowledge was more medieval than modern. The belief was that illness and disease was caused by bad air"

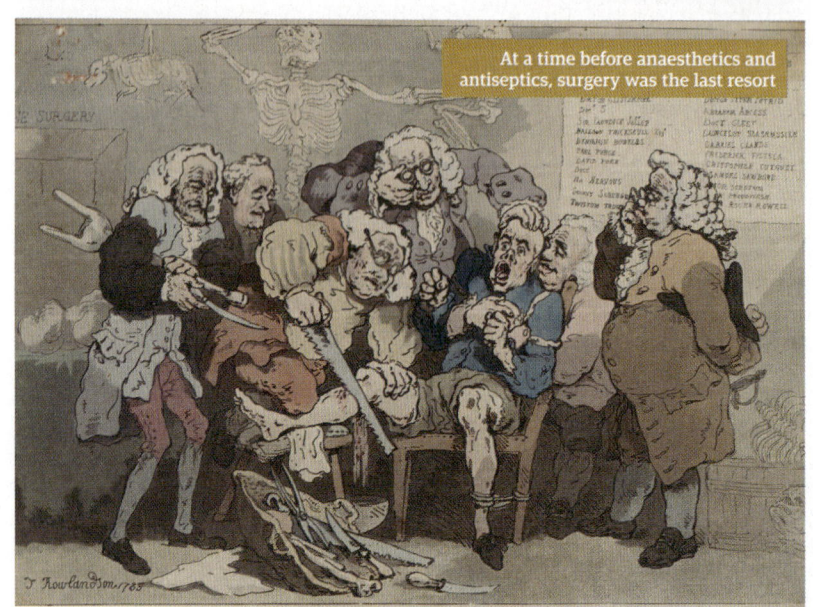

DOCTOR'S ORDERS

THE ANATOMIST.

As well as worrying about the pain of surgery, many thought that doctors were keen to turn operations – and the patients – into medical demonstrations

potent at night, health-conscious people slept with windows shuttered and heavy curtains drawn. If a wealthy person was unlucky enough to fall ill, they'd be sent to the countryside or coast, where the air was thought to be cleaner.

For the unfortunates who couldn't escape to the country at the first sign of a sniffle, the most cost-effective treatment came from an apothecary. Their job was to formulate and dispense medicines – sometimes at the request of a doctor, sometimes on their own initiative. Apothecaries used tinctures and poultices made from herbs, plants and other natural ingredients. One of their favourites was laudanum, a mixture of opium and high-proof alcohol that was used for pain relief and to cure a host of maladies including coughs, colds, meningitis and heart disease.

Although some of the apothecaries' natural medicines may have worked – or at least not made things worse – their ability to provide patients with opium, mercury and other toxic substances meant that unscrupulous or untrained apothecaries often did more harm than good. The government tried to take some control of the unregulated trade with the Apothecaries Act of 1815, which introduced compulsory apprenticeships. All apothecaries required knowledge of anatomy, botany, chemistry and pharmacy, and were required to spend six months gaining practical experience in a hospital.

It's doubtful whether any of these newly trained apothecaries would have been able to ease the suffering of Burney during her mastectomy. She did at least survive, albeit with scars both physical and mental. Hundreds of thousands of fellow patients didn't – because if the illness didn't kill them, the cure probably did.

Frances Burney lived another 29 years after surgery for breast cancer, but never forgot the brutal operation

CULTURE & KNOWLEDGE

REGENCY DISCOVERY AND INNOVATION

During the Regency period, Great Britain became a powerhouse of innovation and science, forging a way into the future

WRITTEN BY **CATHERINE CURZON**

The dawn of the Regency era brought with it a new world of glittering new possibilities, from art and literature to science and innovation. In the wake of the Age of Enlightenment and the Industrial Revolution, as the Britain turned towards the future, the expectant nation was poised for discoveries, and a host of scientists, engineers, naturalists and more were waiting to oblige. From George Stephenson's triumphant locomotive, Blücher, to Mary Anning's remarkable finds as a young girl, it seemed as though anything was possible.

THE DAVY LAMP
A light in dangerous darkness
1815

After several catastrophic explosions in the Northeast collieries, Humphry Davy was invited to develop a way to light collieries safely, ensuring that production could continue without interruption, and that the men who toiled in the mines were safe. With the naked flames of lamps and candles igniting a deadly gas known as firedamp, time was of the essence. Over a three-month period in late 1815, Davy produced several prototypes, trying to light the darkness without igniting the gas. Finally, he settled on a simple but revolutionary design that enclosed the flame in a chimney of wire gauze. This enabled light to permeate, but also absorbed much of the heat, stopping it from igniting any gas present. Davy's lamp was trialed in January 1816 and was soon in every mine, increasing coal production and decreasing fatalities.

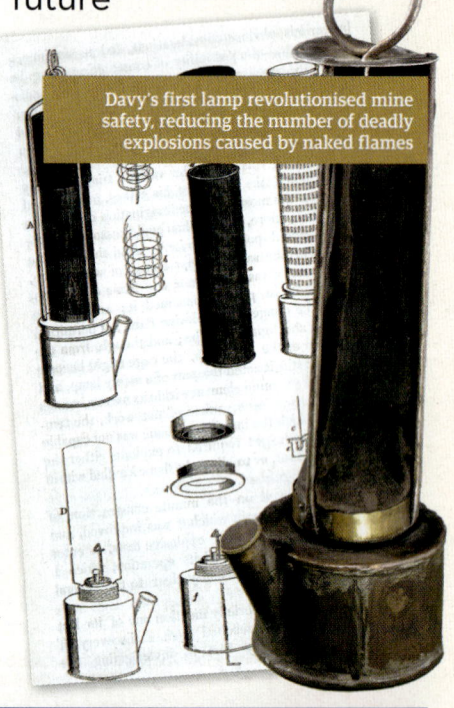

Davy's first lamp revolutionised mine safety, reducing the number of deadly explosions caused by naked flames

The Father of the Railways unveiled Blücher in 1814; it was the first of a long line of Stephenson's locomotives

BLÜCHER THE STEAM ENGINE
It's time to rest the horses...
1814

Named in honour of the Prussian General Blücher, who famously moved with impressive speed in his campaign against Napoleon, George Stephenson's first ever locomotive was designed and built in 1814. Though based on an existing locomotive, Blücher was a significant step forward on anything that had gone before in that it could haul 30 tonnes of coal uphill at a rate of 6kph (4mph). Unlike the horses that usually did the job, the engine would never tire or need to rest, nor would it need to be fed, stabled or fall ill. Developed during Stephenson's tenure at Killingworth Colliery as an engine wright, Blücher was the first in a series of more than a dozen locomotives, each improving on the last. Sadly, Blücher no longer exists, as Stephenson dismantled it to use its parts in future models, while he earned his title of Father of the Railways.

REGENCY DISCOVERY AND INNOVATION

THE HERSCHEL SIBLINGS
Stargazers to royalty
1810-20

In a career that spanned decades, siblings William and Caroline Herschel became famed for their astronomical discoveries, which earned them both recognition and decoration from the crowned heads of Europe. While William enjoyed the honour of being 'the King's astronomer' during the reign of George III, his younger sister, Caroline, received a gold medal for her scientific works from the King of Prussia. Though born in Hanover, the Herschels made their home in England and throughout the Regency era, William made a study of sunspots, speculating on their role in crop management and regional climates; his findings remain in use today. Though Caroline was officially recognised only as her brother's assistant, she was in fact a skilled astronomer in her own right, discovering nebulae, comets and more. In recognition of her skills and expertise, she eventually became the first woman to receive a salary for her scientific work.

The Herschels were an astrology powerhouse, though Caroline was so much more than a mere teamaker

MARY ANNING'S PALEONTOLOGICAL FINDS
Never underestimate a curious girl
1811

When Mary Anning was 12 years old, her brother, Joseph, dug up a 1.2-metre (four-foot) ichthyosaur skull near their home in Lyme Regis, Dorset. A little while later, Mary succeeded in finding the rest of the dinosaur's skeleton. The complete skeleton was sold by Mary's mother, Molly, to local squire Henry Henley for £23 and was the first such discovery ever made. Mary's father earned a supplementary income by selling fossils he had found and, following his death in 1810, her mother continued the business. Mary took on the role of paleontologist, finding specimens for her mother to sell. Among her discoveries were the first complete plesiosaurus and a pterosaur, yet she went mostly unrewarded during her lifetime. Today, however, Anning is lauded as the pioneer she was and has become an inspiration for a whole new generation of young paleontology enthusiasts.

Anning was a paleontological pioneer, unearthing remarkable finds around her Dorset home

THE STEAM-POWERED PRINTING PRESS
A sign of *The Times*
1814

German inventor Friedrich Koenig established a studio in London with Andreas Bauer, where they worked on bringing Koenig's patented steam-powered printing press to life. The design used steam power and rotary cylinders to enable both sides of each page to be printed on at the same time, at an unrivalled speed, far outclassing hand-operated presses. The duo's first customer was *The Times* newspaper, which bought two machines in 1814 in order to print the 29 November issue. Though the printing took place in secret, amid fears that the disgruntled printing press operators might follow the lead of the Luddites and smash the machines, the experiment was a success. Turning out more than 1,000 pages an hour, *The Times* could now outpace its competitors in labour and printing costs, whilst Koenig and Bauer soared to success, with the company still doing business in the global market today.

The Times made history when it employed the first steam-powered printing press to turn out the news

CULTURE & KNOWLEDGE

LIGHTING UP LONDON
Gas brings a blaze to London
1813

Throughout the 1790s, William Murdoch was experimenting with gas as a means of light, which eventually led to him lighting industrial sites. London, meanwhile, had to wait until 1807 to see gas light, when Pall Mall was the first street in the world to have gas-powered lighting in a demonstration of what might one day be possible across the country. However, it would not be until the Regency era that the people of the capital once again turned out to celebrate the wonder of gas-fuelled lights, when the London and Westminster Gas Light and Coke Company illuminated Westminster Bridge on New Year's Eve, 1813. Over the years that followed, more gas lights were lit in the capital, all of them relying on a lamplighter to ensure that they functioned. Other cities would have to wait a decade or more to see gas lights installed in the streets, which changed the face of the country forever.

Not everyone was convinced that gas was the future of London street lighting!

Modern photographers still have much to thank William Hyde Wollaston's meniscus lens for

THE MENISCUS LENS
The photographers' friend
1812

William Hyde Wollaston, who had already gained recognition for the discovery of palladium and rhodium, was not done with innovation by the time of the Regency period. A keen researcher into optical sciences, in 1812 he developed the first lens specifically intended for camera use, the meniscus lens. Inspired by the need to flatten out the distortion of the popular camera obscura, Woolaston's invention was a huge improvement on the lenses already in use and made viewing a far more pleasant experience. The existing biconvex lenses caused significant distortion, whereas Woolaston's concave meniscus lens eliminated most of these flaws, resulting in a flat image. Eventually becoming known as the Wollaston Landscape Lens, the invention far outlasted the popularity of the camera obscura and proved so effective at its task that it was still being used in cameras well into the 20th century.

REGENCY DISCOVERY AND INNOVATION

SARAH GUPPY, BRIDGE BUILDER
The woman whose patent beat Brunel

1811

In 1811, Sarah Guppy became the first woman to patent a bridge design; it was a chain bridge and this, along with her friendship with Isambard Kingdom Brunel, has led to her wrongly being identified as the true designer of the Clifton Suspension Bridge. In fact, Guppy's bridge differed from the design submitted by Brunel in many ways. Unable to file patents in her own name due to her gender, Guppy was nevertheless recognised by her peers for her skills and was more than happy to allow other engineers and inventors to use her patented ideas for their own designs. With little interest in financial profit, she simply wanted to see the designs in use. Guppy's expertise played a part in Thomas Telford's Menai Bridge, and she later became involved in Brunel's SS Great Western, SS Great Britain and the Great Western Railway, offering advice and suggestions as the projects were developed.

Though she didn't design the Clifton Suspension Bridge, Sarah Guppy was a true pioneer

Michael Faraday's voltaic pile was his first recorded experiment; it certainly wasn't his last

THE VOLTAIC PILE
Seven halfpennies can change the world

1812

Celebrated for his work on electricity and magnetism, Michael Faraday's first known experiment was recorded in a letter he wrote on 12 July 1812. In it he described his construction of a voltaic pile using seven halfpennies, stacked together with discs of zinc and paper dampened with salt water. He was then able to pass an electrical current through the pile. The voltaic pile was invented by Italian chemist Alessandro Volta in 1799 and was the first electrical battery able to provide a current via a circuit. Faraday simplified Volta's design and brought the voltaic pile into his other experiments with electricity. In 1814, Faraday and his mentor, Humphry Davy, toured Europe and met Volta. In recognition of Faraday's work, Volta presented him with an example of his own voltaic pile, that which had inspired Faraday's experiment.

THE FIRST HUMAN BLOOD TRANSFUSION
A bloody successful business

1818

In 1818, after seeing too many women dying in childbirth, obstetrician James Blundell proposed that it would be possible to treat severe blood loss during labour with a blood transfusion. After a series of experiments with animals, Blundell was satisfied that it was feasible to successfully transfuse blood even after it had been collected and stored in a container, rather than transferred directly from the donor's vein to that of the recipient. That same year, Blundell performed the first successful human to human transfusion on a married couple, successfully transfusing four ounces of blood from the arm of a man into that of his wife. Many of the instruments he developed remain in use today and it was Blundell who first discovered the vital importance of ensuring that no air remained in the syringe prior to beginning the delicate procedure.

The first human blood transfusion was a revolutionary moment, changing medicine forever

REGENCY BRITAIN

Future PLC Quay House, The Ambury, Bath, BA1 1UA

Editorial
Editor **Jessica Leggett**
Senior Designer **Philip Martin**
Head of Art & Design **Greg Whitaker**
Editorial Director **Jon White**
Managing Director **Grainne McKenna**

All About History Editorial
Editor **Jonathan Gordon**
Art Editor **Thomas Parrett**
Editorial Director **Tim Williamson**
Senior Art Editor **Duncan Crook**

Contributors
Catherine Curzon, Nell Darby, Mark Dolan, Paul Edwards, Tom Garner, Jonathan Gordon, James Hoare, Robert Lock, Callum McKelvie, Scott Reeves, Emma Slattery Williams, Emily Staniforth

Cover images
Alamy, Getty Images, Wikimedia Commons

Photography
All copyrights and trademarks are recognised and respected

Advertising
Media packs are available on request
Commercial Director **Clare Dove**

International
Head of Print Licensing **Rachel Shaw**
licensing@futurenet.com
www.futurecontenthub.com

Circulation
Head of Newstrade **Tim Mathers**

Production
Head of Production **Mark Constance**
Production Project Manager **Matthew Eglinton**
Advertising Production Manager **Joanne Crosby**
Digital Editions Controller **Jason Hudson**
Production Managers **Keely Miller, Nola Cokely, Vivienne Calvert, Fran Twentyman**

Printed in the UK

Distributed by Marketforce – www.marketforce.co.uk
For enquiries, please email: mfcommunications@futurenet.com

Book of Regency Britain First Edition (AHB6375)
© 2024 Future Publishing Limited

We are committed to only using magazine paper which is derived from responsibly managed, certified forestry and chlorine-free manufacture. The paper in this bookazine was sourced and produced from sustainable managed forests, conforming to strict environmental and socioeconomic standards.

All contents © 2024 Future Publishing Limited or published under licence. All rights reserved. No part of this magazine may be used, stored, transmitted or reproduced in any way without the prior written permission of the publisher. Future Publishing Limited (company number 2008885) is registered in England and Wales. Registered office: Quay House, The Ambury, Bath BA1 1UA. All information contained in this publication is for information only and is, as far as we are aware, correct at the time of going to press. Future cannot accept any responsibility for errors or inaccuracies in such information. You are advised to contact manufacturers and retailers directly with regard to the price of products/services referred to in this publication. Apps and websites mentioned in this publication are not under our control. We are not responsible for their contents or any other changes or updates to them. This magazine is fully independent and not affiliated in any way with the companies mentioned herein.

FUTURE Connectors. Creators. Experience Makers.

Future plc is a public company quoted on the London Stock Exchange (symbol: FUTR)
www.futureplc.com

Chief Executive Officer **Jon Steinberg**
Non-Executive Chairman **Richard Huntingford**
Chief Financial Officer **Sharjeel Suleman**

Tel +44 (0)1225 442 244

Part of the

ALL ABOUT HISTORY
bookazine series

Widely Recycled | ipso. Regulated